getting real about
urbanism
CONTEXTUAL DESIGN
FOR CITIES

BERNARD ZYSCOVICH, AIA
with Douglas R. Porter, FAICP

**Urban Land
Institute**

ULI–the Urban Land Institute
1025 Thomas Jefferson Street, N.W.
Suite 500 West
Washington, D.C. 20007-5201

Library of Congress Cataloging-in-Publication Data

Zyscovich, Bernard.
  Getting real about urbanism : contextual design for cities / Bernard Zyscovich with Douglas R. Porter.
     p. cm.
  ISBN 978-0-87420-105-5 (alk. paper)
  1. Urban renewal. 2. City planning. I. Porter, Douglas R. II. Title.
  HT170.Z97 2008
  307.760973–dc22

                    2008035904

10 9 8 7 6 5 4 3 2 1
Printed in the United States of America.

© **Mixed Sources**
Product group from well-managed
forests, controlled sources and
recycled wood or fiber
www.fsc.org Cert no. SW-COC-002669
© 1996 Forest Stewardship Council

THE MISSION of the Urban Land Institute is to provide leadership in the responsible use of land and in creating and sustaining thriving communities worldwide. ULI is committed to

- Bringing together leaders from across the fields of real estate and land use policy to exchange best practices and serve community needs;
- Fostering collaboration within and beyond ULI's membership through mentoring, dialogue, and problem solving;
- Exploring issues of urbanization, conservation, regeneration, land use, capital formation, and sustainable development;
- Advancing land use policies and design practices that respect the uniqueness of both built and natural environments;
- Sharing knowledge through education, applied research, publishing, and electronic media; and
- Sustaining a diverse global network of local practice and advisory efforts that address current and future challenges.

Established in 1936, the Institute today has more than 40,000 members worldwide, representing the entire spectrum of the land use and development disciplines. ULI relies heavily on the experience of its members. It is through member involvement and information resources that ULI has been able to set standards of excellence in development practice. The Institute has long been recognized as one of the world's most respected and widely quoted sources of objective information on urban planning, growth, and development.

project staff

Rachelle L. Levitt
Executive Vice President
Global Information Group
Publisher

Dean Schwanke
Senior Vice President
Publications and Awards

Adrienne Schmitz
Senior Director, Residential
   and Community Development
Project Director

Kathryn Terzano
Associate, Information

Jacob Arem
Intern

Nancy H. Stewart
Director, Book Program
Managing Editor

Lise Lingo
Publications Professionals LLC
Manuscript Editor

Betsy VanBuskirk
Creative Director

Craig Chapman
Director, Publishing Operations

John Hall Design Group
Beverly, Massachusetts
Book and Cover Design

Bernard Zyscovich

As managing principal of Zyscovich Architects, in Miami, Florida, Bernard Zyscovich, AIA, leads his firm of over 120 people in probing the parameters of design innovation. A dedicated urbanist, Zyscovich is committed to design that reinforces the cultural, commercial, and recreational opportunities of the urban fabric. He has given lectures on his theories of real urbanism to a variety of groups around the United States and his writing on architecture and urban design has been published in numerous magazines. Zyscovich received his bachelor of architecture degree from Pratt Institute in 1971.

Douglas R. Porter

Douglas Porter, FAICP, is president of the Growth Management Institute in Chevy Chase, Maryland. His work bridges traditional specialties in urban planning and development, from affordable housing to transit-oriented development, city and regional growth strategies, urban design and redevelopment, citizen involvement, and green infrastructure. He has authored many books and articles and frequently lectures on these topics. Previously he directed public policy research at the Urban Land Institute and was a principal of a planning consulting firm. He has degrees in urban and regional planning from Michigan State University and the University of Illinois.

BEING A PRACTICING ARCHITECT focused on the creative acts of urban planning and architecture, my most appreciative thanks are for my friend and coach Laura Cerwinske. Laura, an accomplished writer in her own right, encouraged me to organize my process and develop the ideas and get them written down on paper. I would like to thank Delma Iles, for enduring and participating in the verbal processing of observations and lessons learned of urban realities during years of what otherwise for couples would be known as vacation. I would also like

acknowledgments

to thank my partners in the firm, Jose Murguido, Anabella Smith, and Suria Yaffar, who supported my efforts in this endeavor without ever questioning the reason or the benefits to the firm. Their unequivocal endorsement of the investigation into urban reasoning for its own sake was a powerful impetus for diving deeper into this exploration. Suria, especially, has been my source of energy and devotion toward this topic because of her own innate and thorough understanding of these issues. She is truly my equal partner in the development of these ideas.

This book would not have been possible without Cheryl Jacobs, who brought these concepts to the attention of ULI, where we had the opportunity to make the pitch. And of course, thanks go to Rachelle Levitt and Adrienne Schmitz, who helped at ULI in the birth and culmination of this effort. In addition, Doug Porter, who has written several books for ULI, was instrumental in the writing of this one.

I would also like to thank the wonderful architects and planners in our urban design studio who have assisted in analyzing and testing these ideas. A special thank-you to Trent Baughn, Melissa Hege, Leslie Sanchez, Manny del Monte, Marcela Cajiao, and Demetrius Carter.

—*Bernard Zyscovich*

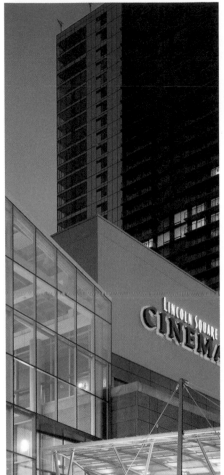

contents

FOR MANY DECADES, the emphasis in planning for new development in cities has been focused on the assertion that we must distill the principles of urban design into a uniform and compact set of rules that can be applied universally. The new urbanism can then be codified into regulations that reinforce this simple and standardized formula.

The purpose of this book is to offer an alternative voice in support of enhancing and creating places that have identifiable character and per-

preface

sonality. I call this point of view "real" urbanism because it is a search for an authentic response to the issues of planning and developing in the urban context. This is not a utopian approach; rather, it consciously searches for the distinctive characteristics of a place without prejudgments or expectations about design solutions.

Real urbanism seeks what is unique and original in any neighborhood, district, city, and region. It recognizes that planning for the redesign of existing places must address the origin and history of those places. It is a contextual and layered approach to creating a plan that reflects the economic and social underpinnings unique to that community in that place and time.

Contextual urban design—which I view as real urbanism—proposes a method for creating flourishing places, using principles based on the discovery and application of their fundamental characteristics. The process encourages creativity and exploration; its rewards are livable and exciting cities for residents and visitors of all ages, incomes, and backgrounds.

—*Bernard Zyscovich*

Opposite: Del Mar Station, Pasadena, California

Photo: Moule & Polyzoides

getting real about urbanism

CITIES AND MATURING SUBURBS across America are participating in a remarkable resurgence of urban livability. Following decades in which historically robust cities withered from within and lackluster suburbs spread into the countryside, urban areas are blooming anew. Residents in many cities and maturing suburban jurisdictions are witnessing the rejuvenation of seemingly worn-out neighborhoods and commercial centers and the energetic actions of developers vying

1 design for urbanism

to instill excitement and verve in once-somnolent suburban venues. Designers are rediscovering ways to create vital living and working environments—places that interweave expressions of history with prized urban qualities.

Experience around the globe tells us that cities live by continuously evolving—conserving and building on memorable features while adapting to changing social and economic circumstances. Elizabeth Barlow Rogers, founder of the Cityscape Institute, put it this way:

> Time means change. Cities and the uses of land within them are both dynamic and stationary, forever being transformed while at the same time maintaining discernible outlines of their original plans. Over time, any city resembles a three-dimensional document in which the primary text has been partially erased, added to, and otherwise amended.[1]

Population growth propels many such changes in the urban scene. Between 2000 and 2008, the U.S. population increased by 20 million people, to more than 300 million. The U.S. Census Bureau projects that by 2050 it will reach 420 million. Almost 90 percent of new U.S. residents are expected to remain in or move to metropolitan areas—clustering within cities and their suburbs. Indeed, according to some students of

urban growth, our concentrations of cities and suburbs are merging into 20 "megapolitan" areas and by 2050 will have consolidated into ten megaregions, five east and five west of the 100th meridian.[2] In all probability the megaregions will grow denser, posing challenges to designers seeking to enhance the increasingly urban quality of life.

People's visions of their desired lifestyles are also significant factors in shaping tomorrow's cities. Where once the nuclear family of two parents and two or more kids was the norm, today such families represent only a quarter of all households. Single adults, married couples, single-parent families, and unrelated groups make up the rest. Some consider this trend a loss of the sensibility of a previous era, but in reality it provides opportunities to accommodate a widening set of living choices. And when demographics change, societies find new interests and out-

Atelier|505 in Boston, Massachusetts, transformed an underutilized, contaminated 1.16-acre (0.47-ha) site into a vibrant 24-hour center of activity and provided the city with its first new performing arts theater in more than 70 years.

Photo: Anton Grassl

Located in a historic precinct of downtown Toronto, Ontario, Canada's National Ballet School (NBS)/Radio City Development is an urban infill project that includes high density housing— two towers and a row of townhouses—as well as an arts training institution, all on a 2.4-acre (1-ha) site. Contemporary architectural expression was emphasized while respecting and foregrounding the existing heritage fabric.

Photos: Eduard Hueber (above) and Tom Arban (opposite)

lets for living. People's housing needs and patterns of work and play generate desires for a broad variety of living environments.

The combination of burgeoning and changing metropolitan populations generates greater demands for development—of shelter, work places, shopping areas, civic services, and infrastructure. Urban change is in the air and visible, too, on the ground. People are taking note of urban design qualities as never before. Hence the remarkable kaleidoscope of stirring urban designs in so many places these days. In response to market demands sensed by real estate developers, designers are broadening the spectrum of opportunities for urban lifestyles, aided in recent decades by their avid experimentation with design forms, concern for sustainability, and increased appreciation of historic examples around the world. "Lifestyle" retail centers that combine shopping with leisure activities, residential developments comprising numerous housing types for a variety of households, and clusters of homes around protected natural areas suggest the multiplicity of designs for living that are becoming common.

Vital Places

Taking cues from the surroundings of their projects, urban designers are increasingly willing to move beyond a placid acceptance of established rules to incorporate a wealth of sensations and even a touch of anarchy in their works. They recognize a modern preference for introducing stimulation and animation in surroundings as a foil for laid-back, subdued reflection. Through design, they seek to reinforce the individuality of places rather than impose prescriptive boundaries on choices. These times of ever-changing living environments call for urban design approaches that conjure vitality as a central motif of urban places.

Many designers today hope to reach that goal by recapturing past visions of high-quality urban design in the United States. Some of their concepts recall the precepts of the City Beautiful movement that blossomed in the late 19th century, stimulated by the 1893 World's Columbian Exposition in Chicago. Besides showing off dramatic

technological advances, the incredibly popular Exposition—it attracted 47 million visitors—demonstrated to Americans the revelatory prospects for enhancing the culture of cities in an increasingly powerful nation: impressive civic complexes, grand thoroughfares, and extensive parks and gardens for city dwellers' enjoyment. Urban designers such as Frederick Law Olmsted, who was responsible for creating New York's

SouthSide Works, in Pittsburgh, is an example of combining residences with retail, leisure, and other activities in a pedestrian-friendly urban environment. The South Side neighborhood has undergone a real revitalization in recent years, spurred by the SouthSide Works project.

Photo: Soffer Organization

Classic urban landscapes—such as those made up by the Victorian homes, parks, and high rises of San Francisco—serve as inspirations for designers seeking to create memorable and livable places today.

Photo: Zyscovich

Central Park, fashioned distinctive settings for urban life in the nation's fast-growing cities. Many designers now strive to emulate these grand masters' convictions about creating memorable urban places that celebrate civic virtues—a hallmark of contextual, or real urbanism.

Other designers attempt to reproduce the neighborly groups of houses and shops clustered around green spaces in small towns across the nation or the close-knit neighborhoods of mature cities ordered by grid street patterns. Many recent developments have featured the vernacular housing, neighborhood, and shopping districts of the 18th and 19th centuries—often charming in detail, but increasingly copied with mindless imitation. Many designers of such developments adhere to a model of urbanism that lays down rules about physical and visual character, such as the design and arrangement of windows in a building and the proximity of buildings to streets, without recognizing the special character of the location or allowing the possibility of variations on the theme. Michael Pyatok, a California-based architect, criticizes many such plans as "picturesque set designs

The redevelopment of the Laurel Homes public housing project in Cincinnati, Ohio, replaces inward-focused superblocks with a pedestrian-friendly grid of tree-lined streets and houses with front porches to foster a sense of community.

Photo: Steve Hall

Laurel Homes contains a variety of structures with varying heights, styles, and setbacks to create an attractive, lively, and safe neighborhood.

Photo: Steve Hall

empty of the physical supports that encourage organic or spontaneous economic and social arrangements."[3] (Oddly, also, many of these urban designs are planted in rural places that have meager associations with real cities and towns.)

A more authentic approach to urban design avoids prescriptive, ideological stances that hobble creativity; rather, it embraces a range of expressive responses to the historical and contextual ambience of specific sites. Urban design springs from the substrata of our culture. Designers planning developments in urban places need to seek out the roots of the contemporary city, which nurture its identity. They must reach back to study the origins and evolutionary layers of communities while looking forward to evaluate new possibilities.

For example, in planning for the redevelopment of the former Laurel Homes public housing project in Cincinnati as a HOPE VI mixed-income residential neighborhood, Torti-Gallas and Partners found that the public housing development had ripped up a historic grid of tree-lined streets and laid out inward-focused superblocks, effectively isolating the project from the surrounding area. Restoring the grid street plan and borrowing the 19th-century Italianate architectural details of nearby historic homes for the new residences, the firm shaped a reconstruction plan that has guided the creation of an attractive, livable neighborhood.

Contextual design pays attention to the framework of new development in a multidimensional way—reflecting a consciousness not only of the surrounding urban scene but also of the evolution of the area over time, the economic and financial stakes involved, and the contributions of physical and social aspects to the built environment. The Clipper Mill project in Baltimore, Maryland, addressed these concerns when the developers undertook the reuse of a five-building complex once devoted to machine manufacturing. Not only did the designers create 168 wonderful living spaces within the formerly decrepit buildings, but they also fashioned studio space to attract the artists and craftspeople who once lived in the area, installed a green roof on one building, used porous paving to mitigate harmful runoff, and reused antique steel beams and sprocket wheels as ornamental features. When recognized as opportunities, contextual elements can underscore the continuity in the dynamic process of city building.

The Clipper Mill project in Baltimore, Maryland, transformed an abandoned industrial complex into a thriving, mixed-use, transit-oriented community, bringing more residents into this part of the city.

Photo: Patrick Ross Photography

Authentic urban design extends beyond a building or project design. It embraces the important roles of community infrastructure systems and public regulatory guidance in enhancing diversity and richness in city and suburban environments. For example, the design for Cincinnati's Laurel Homes HOPE VI project transformed the right-of-way of a major water main into a linear park and preserved a cluster of old trees as green space. The famous revival of Baltimore's waterfront into a lively destination for residents and visitors was directed by guidelines that were established in a widely respected urban design plan.

In summary, the core principles of contextual urbanism advocate

- Discovering the origins of the current conditions and inventing new possibilities that anticipate taking urban evolution to a new level;
- Promoting new visions and pathways to celebrate urban life, sparking redevelopment in infill areas, transforming areas that need reinvestment, and establishing a sense of place and urban vitality in lackluster centers and neighborhoods;
- Focusing on a process rather than a formula, reaching back in time to understand the historic values and ongoing trends in areas affected by stress and change;
- Creating dynamic connections that generate value for the physical, visual, and economic contexts of proposed designs;

Clipper Mill site plan.

Graphic: Bill Shinn & Associates

- Broadening the spectrum of opportunities for residence, employment, means of transportation, recreation, and culture to maximize the vitality and excitement of urban living;
- Relating public with private interests, business with residential and civic activities, and development with sound community infrastructure systems; and
- Creating urban designs unique to the moment and place, expressing individuality and tolerance of difference and variety while satisfying real needs and desires.

Creating Contextual Design in an Area of Disinvestment

The development plan for a mixed-use project in the heart of Miami, Florida, illustrates how one development project has reflected the community's legacy and the site's context in the project's form and features. The creation of Midtown Miami grew out of the city's larger concern for revitalizing an 85-block, 1,400-acre (567-ha), underdeveloped corridor in the Bayfront area, just north of the new Adrienne Arsht Center for the Performing Arts and next to downtown. City officials were intensely concerned about promoting opportunities for business and job expansion

Lincoln Square in Bellevue, Washington, is a 1.4 million-square-foot (130,000-sq-m) mixed-use project that has been widely credited as being a catalyst for further development in the urban core of this first-tier suburb of Seattle.

Photo: Mark Silverstein

Aerial images show the former container yard that was transformed into Midtown Miami in Miami, Florida. The plan calls for a mix of uses, densities, and styles to create an urban setting and revitalize a neighborhood in the heart of the city and includes provisions for a streetcar.

Graphic: Zyscovich

in the area, as well as improving the livability of some of Miami's oldest and most diverse neighborhoods. The corridor parallels the Florida East Coast Railway (FEC) line along Biscayne Bay and contains both gentrified and economically depressed neighborhoods and a scattering of office, retail, and light industrial uses. An economic analysis by Florida International University's Metropolitan Center found that the residents' demands for goods and services within the market area were underserved but the area's central location was conducive to the expansion of business and jobs.

The city commissioned Zyscovich Architects to prepare the urban design component of the FEC strategic redevelopment plan. The firm began by evaluating each neighborhood's historic and current economic and cultural vitality and then structured a plan to capitalize on the opportunities for change and improvement in the various areas. The plan calls for low-rise development along the bayfront, bordered by high-rise, mixed-use development on the other side of Biscayne Boulevard. A parallel trolley line (along a historic trolley route) and a walking/biking linear park will tie the neighborhoods together and provide much quicker access to downtown than did the existing bus lines. At the northern end, another business and greenway corridor was planned to generate business revitalization and expansion.

Early in the planning studies, we pinpointed a 56-acre (23-ha) parcel used by the FEC for container storage as an opportune site for sparking revitalization. A blighting influence, the brownfield property was fenced off from the neighboring areas and disrupted the city's street grid. The plan proposed developing the site for high density and a mix of uses as a centerpiece of the urban design strategy. The FEC's initial reluctance to sell the property was eventually overcome by the city's intense concern for furthering revitalization of this key sector of the city and by its commitment to implementing the redevelopment plan. Biscayne Development Partners acquired the property and immediately turned to us to oversee a design plan for the development, named Midtown Miami.

At Midtown Miami, ground-floor retail and high-rise structures are oriented to the street and are designed to encourage pedestrian activity.

Graphic: Zyscovich

Above and opposite: Midtown
Miami incorporates a mix
of high- and low-rise towers
and lies along the route of a
proposed trolley line.

Photos: New York Focus

We began by reestablishing a grid street system linked to the surrounding area, framed by North Miami Avenue on the west and the railway on the east and including a central landscaped boulevard along the
length of the project. Development projected for the site included 3,000
condominium units, 150,000 square feet (14,000 sq m) of office space,
and 140,000 square feet (13,000 sq m) of commercial space. High-
rise residential and office buildings were to be concentrated along the
east side, facing lower-rise structures along the west side. The plan
called for ground-floor retail space that would enliven the district's
street life and for carefully designed parking structures, architecturally
blended into the upper floors of buildings. The plan also included detailed
design guidelines and a block-by-block tailoring of permitted uses and
building height, bulk, and placement.

But these requirements do not hinder diversity. The urban design plan
for Midtown Miami proposed a development program for creating a wide
range of building types suited to the desired mix of uses and planned to
create an exciting, authentic, urban experience. The first three condominium buildings were each designed by different architects and look very
different. The retail development incorporates both high-end merchandise

and services and more modest outlets catering to lower-income neighborhood residents. It is far from a one-size-fits-all environment; instead it provides a place for many activities and many kinds of people. The improved street system and proposed trolley line along the length of the corridor establish connections among the various activities.

As of early 2008, Developers Diversified Realty had completed a 645,000-square-foot (60,000-sq-m) retail center, the Shops of Midtown Miami, plus 900 rental apartments and a 2,000-car parking garage, on a 26-acre (10.5-ha) site bordered on the west by North Miami Avenue and on the north by 36th Street. Meanwhile, The Midtown Group developed 3,000 residential units in three buildings along Midtown Boulevard, two of which are occupied. The buildings include rent-to-own as well as for-sale units. Midtown Miami, an example of carefully considered contextual design, is well on its way to revitalizing business activity and residential neighborhoods in the FEC area.

Overview of the Book

The gestation of the Midtown Miami plan describes the realistic approach to urban design that is the central subject of this book. The book spells out, chapter by chapter, the principal elements of the creative process for designing authentically urban development in a contextual framework. The chapters describe exemplary developments that illustrate specific applications of this design concept in a wide variety of urban environments.

Chapter 2, "Urban Design in Context," details the essential elements that urban designers must consider in creating projects. It also demonstrates how elements of contextual urbanism, which build on concepts of smart growth, can be adapted to produce invigorating designs for development in stagnant or deteriorating areas as well as in growing areas.

Chapter 3, "Sustainable, Green Urbanism," describes how designers pursuing the goals of authentic urban design can also implement significant aspects of sustainable and green development by capitalizing on the historic and contextual advantages of sites and areas. Examples illustrate sustainability and green features in specific projects.

Chapter 4, "The Discovery Process," explains research procedures for determining key site and neighborhood features and design approaches to resolving issues of concern to stakeholders. It also gives examples of practices for synthesizing design ideas to meet community objectives.

Opposite: The Miami Beach Art Deco District's "main street," Ocean Drive, establishes the architectural template for the neighborhood.

Photo: Steven Brooke

Chapter 5, "Public Framework and Vision" underscores the need to frame designs, illustrations, and guidelines that identify key public interventions and reconsiderations in the design process and that include recognition of opportunities that will ensure success, including regulatory tools for phased implementation of designs.

Chapter 6, "Toward Real Urbanism," reiterates the importance of anchoring development in a local context while respecting the natural, historical, built, and human environments and building strong communities.

By studying the examples and applying the strategies described in this book, urban designers can help to bring about better, more authentic urban forms and create more livable and sustainable urban environments.

1 Elizabeth Barlow Rogers, *Reclaiming the High Line* (New York: Design Trust for Public Space, Inc., 2002), p. 20.

2 Robert E. Lang and Arthur C. Nelson, "Super Regions to Serve Super Growth," in Douglas R. Porter, *Managing Growth in Urban America,* 2nd edition (Washington, D.C.: Island Press, 2007), p. 7.

3 Quoted by Mark Hinshaw in "True Urbanism," *Planning,* June 2005, p. 25.

THE PRACTICE OF URBAN DESIGN seeks to integrate a broad range of activities that contribute vitality to urban environments. Vital places provide opportunities for people to connect and interact as they conduct business, provide services, enjoy leisure activities, absorb information, and live as households. Even in this age of electronic communication, people benefit—and communities gain—from the face-to-face encounters encouraged by urban settings. Experience shows that certain

2 urban design in context

age-old characteristics of cities and towns can facilitate these relationships and, at the same time, provide wonderful visual venues that heighten people's enjoyment of their activities. The classic cities of antiquity and even small towns laid out in the American wilderness provided a beneficial proximity, enabling residents to satisfy many needs within a small area.

Harbor Town in Memphis, Tennessee, is a planned community on the banks of the Mississippi River, across from downtown Memphis. Its design emphasizes compact development and a diverse mix of uses.

Photo: Jim Hilliard
Aerial Photography

Even the "cowtowns" that were constructed almost overnight on the plains and mountainsides of western states clustered buildings together for convenience, security, and profit.

To achieve real urbanism, these age-old characteristics must become key objectives of the urban design process. While many households still prefer homes in suburban neighborhoods that leave owners dependent on travel by cars, increasing numbers now trade distance for the convenience of proximity. They are willing—even eager—to participate in urban life, amid built environments that offer a variety of activities and visual experiences. They like living within walking distance of destinations that are significant in their everyday lives.

The residents of Harbor Town have added to the vibrancy of downtown Memphis.

Photo: Jeffrey Jacobs/
Mims Studios

Guiding Principles for Creating Urbanism

The design of truly urban development focuses on creating buildings, complexes, neighborhoods, and centers that respond to widely accepted guiding principles. The key elements of urbanism spring from several

sources that reflect a remarkable convergence of opinion in recent years about the fundamental tenets of urban design. After the City Beautiful movement of the 1890s brought the topic to the national table for discussion, countless master plans for cities across the United States propounded lists of goals and principles for guiding future growth. Typically these plans called for directing growth to areas served or able to be served efficiently by infrastructure systems and public facilities; taking steps to revitalize rundown areas and improve housing conditions; and conserving natural land resources. Since the 1980s, advocates for improving urban livability have proposed other lists of principles describing the optimal planning and design characteristics of urban development, such as smart growth, neo-traditional development, new urbanism, and transit-oriented development.

These lists coalesce around eight guiding principles for urban development that are strongly reflected in the precepts of true urbanism:

- Compact development of the built environment;
- Diversity of uses, activity centers, and neighborhoods;
- Range of housing, employment, and lifestyle opportunities;
- Variety of transportation choices and walkable neighborhoods;
- Efficient provision of infrastructure and public services;
- Distinctive communities with a strong sense of place;
- Preserved green spaces, farmland, and natural features and ecosystems;
- Fair, predictable, and cost-effective development decisions based on community involvement and collaboration.[1]

To this list, aspects of green development are now being added to promote sustainability. These elements (discussed in chapter 3), such as energy efficiency, waste management and recycling, materials reuse, and water management, pertain to individual buildings, development projects, and neighborhoods and communities.

COMPACT DEVELOPMENT

"Compact" means "closely united or collected" or "concentrated in a small area." Compact development puts buildings and activities closer together so that they occupy less land than conventional development. Although compactness suggests rather dense development, both compactness and density are relative terms, not absolutes. They describe levels of development that are appropriate for the location and the market. What may be labeled moderate density in some places may be viewed as high density in others. Compactness treats land as a valuable resource to be

A variety of architecture can help create neighborhood character.

Photo: Thorn Grafton

The redevelopment of the Flamingo rental complex in Miami Beach, Florida, added a tower to a mid-rise complex which also includes a marina and a retail center.

Photo: Zyscovich

used efficiently, and the resulting proximity of various activities is viewed as an asset. Density can also add value to existing properties by creating synergies of use and activity.

Cities make compactness a virtue. Urban forms of development gather people together in homes and shops, in work places and civic spaces, to improve opportunities for sheltering, working, shopping, learning, worshipping, and other requirements of daily life. Higher densities create activity centers and neighborhoods that look and feel different from spread-out suburban developments, and the difference generates social as well as economic value. Compactly developed areas attract people who enjoy being in places that offer convenient access to shops, services, and cultural life. In return, their patronage energizes and nourishes a broad range of activities that create the "theater of the street" as a source of continually available entertainment.

But getting compactness right requires fine-grained design that not only is attuned to the market but also creates an attractive context for everyday encounters. Many Americans picture densely developed areas as unsightly or alien—drab, if not shabby, congested, and architecturally jumbled, with unattractive buildings that diminish the quality of urban life. Yet many of today's urban designers have gained considerable experience in shaping attractive groupings of structures and lively streetscapes that create appealing environments for living, leisure, and work. They merge historic and contemporary styles, wrap new buildings next to old ones, and create magical opportunities for establishing a more enjoyable environment. Density, even in places with massive structures, captures the contemporary imagination when it extends the legacy of the past. Height can provide a satisfying alternative to uninterrupted mass. Tall buildings can allow greater penetration of light and air to the street than the continuous walls of lower, extended buildings. A well-designed tower can animate a skyline, becoming a signature of a city's aesthetic vitality. Even a huge structure can be animated with varying volumes that set up interesting visual and spatial rhythms.

Diverse uses have made the Flamingo rental complex an urban oasis and helped revitalize the surrounding neighborhood.

Photo: Zyscovich

The Flamingo rental complex for retirees on a 16.5-acre (6.7-ha) waterfront site in Miami's South Beach, exemplifies the mix of building sizes and shapes that creates attractive urban development. The Flamingo originally comprised two Y-shaped mid-rise buildings constructed in the 1960s. Despite the site's proximity to downtown Miami and the waterfront, the development lacked appeal and its owner, AIMCO, sought to increase the site's value through further development. After analyzing the property's potential development under zoning and regulatory processes, Zyscovich Architects determined that a tower and hundreds of new units could be added to the site, leading AIMCO to propose construction of a new residential tower in addition to upgrades to the two existing buildings. We suggested repositioning the complex as a 21st-century, full-service, rental resort. Ultimately the Flamingo became one of the most successful urban revitalization developments in South Beach.

The design focused on developing an urban oasis combining relatively high density, a diverse mix of uses, green space and pedestrian paths, and parking, all of which have brought 24-hour activity to the development. The plan called for increasing unit sizes in the existing towers and constructing a new 32-story, 463-unit tower. This elliptical, stand-alone structure has a much smaller footprint than the original Y-shaped apartment buildings. The new tower's position as a pivot point within the site helped integrate both social and physical aspects of the development. The design also incorporated 24 garden apartments; 28 townhouses surrounding a seven-story, 2,000-car garage; and substantial amenities: a two-acre (0.8-ha) botanical park, a 14,000-square-foot (1,300-sq-m) state-of-the-art gym, a marina, swimming pools, and a mall-like marketplace. The plan demonstrated to city officials and the public that a large residential property can provide a variety of opportunities to create a lively, truly urban, mixed-use environment.

Density need not be achieved with tall buildings, however. Compactness is a matter of context—the density of nearby development—and can be realized with closely spaced buildings of relatively modest heights. Bethesda Row, in a Maryland suburb of Washington, D.C., combines mostly three-story retail and office buildings with an eight-story residential structure. It expands a maturing regional activity center with an exciting and compact mix of interactive uses and includes reuse of old buildings as well as new structures.

Since the 1980s, much of downtown Bethesda has been reconstructed, with substantial office, retail, and residential development focused around a Metrorail station. Bethesda Row, encompassing new and existing buildings, wrapped the retail frontages and a condominium

Opposite: The downtown area of Bethesda, Maryland, has been revitalized by the development of Bethesda Row, a higher-density, mixed-use center with plentiful greenery and outdoor seating.

Photo: Cooper Carry

building around a large county-owned parking structure. The retail streetscapes are planted with trees and other landscaping and feature broad, brick-paved sidewalks with space for seating and outdoor dining. Bethesda Row's development exemplifies design of a scale and place-making quality that has generated strong patronage in an affluent community and stimulated plans for further development on nearby parcels.

Another example is Legacy at Museum Park, an urban infill development in San Jose, California, which comprises 117 rental housing units on a 3.38-acre (1.37-ha) site. Rather than gather all the units in one or two apartment buildings, architects Meeks + Partners drew a plan for 11 distinct buildings that moderated the impression of density and corresponded in scale with surrounding developments. The project includes flats, townhouses, and live/work lofts, and the design varies the building features according to the type of unit. Flats are paired with townhouses, with two flats over clustered garages adjacent to two townhouses. The flats are in three-story, garden-style walkup buildings with balconies or decks. The townhouses have pitched roofs, gable windows, and the

raised entry stoops typical of urban rowhouses of the early 1900s. The live/work lofts are in two- and three-story structures with flat roofs, large storefront-like windows, and ceiling heights up to 19 feet (5.8 m). Bringing the buildings right up to the sidewalk allowed enough room on the site to build one- and two-car garages, most with direct access to the units. Guest parking is provided along internal loop streets. The variety of units and structures provides a broad mix of sizes and rent levels, which not only makes for a diverse community but also expands the market of potential renters.[2]

DIVERSITY OF ACTIVITIES

Throughout the ages, cities have been built by mixing a variety of uses next to one another as a matter of course. Such a development pattern serves pedestrians well because people can easily walk from home to work to shopping, and so on. While the mix allows related activities to exist near each other, it can also adapt to changing circumstances. The mix often included combined retail and residential uses, with business owners even living in apartments above their businesses. The evolution

Legacy at Museum Park, in San Jose, California, is an urban infill development helping to fulfill the area's great need for multifamily housing.

Photo: Meeks + Partners

of zoning in the 20th century changed all that. Euclidian zoning—so named because of its origins in Euclid, Ohio—was invented to protect residents and workers from the ill effects of noxious land uses, particularly dirty, noisy industrial activity. Cities adopted ordinances that zoned large parcels of territory for single uses—specific types of housing, local or regional retailing, manufacturing, and so on. But after several decades of trial and error, more and more city officials have come to realize that this approach fails to produce the kinds of communities that they wanted to achieve; producing those communities requires stirring in various uses to help create more interesting and functional environments. Developers agreed to add services, citing consumer demands for convenient access; as a result, most zoning ordinances now incorporate options to develop commercial and office centers with residential and recreational components, and vice versa. Some even allow certain types of clean industrial uses.

For designers, the growing inclusiveness of zoning practices provides opportunities for enriching the urban texture. By fostering anticipation and possibilities for unexpected encounters, diversity generates a more stimulating visual environment. Writer and urban critic Roberta Brandes Gratz said it well: "Cities, towns, neighborhoods, and commercial districts should be unpredictable. . .and idiosyncratic, shaped by the unexpected and colorful, and as interesting as life itself."[3] Contextual design

Urban row townhomes with stoops and patios were included in Legacy at Museum Park to stimulate the neighborhood with pedestrian traffic.

Photo: Meeks + Partners

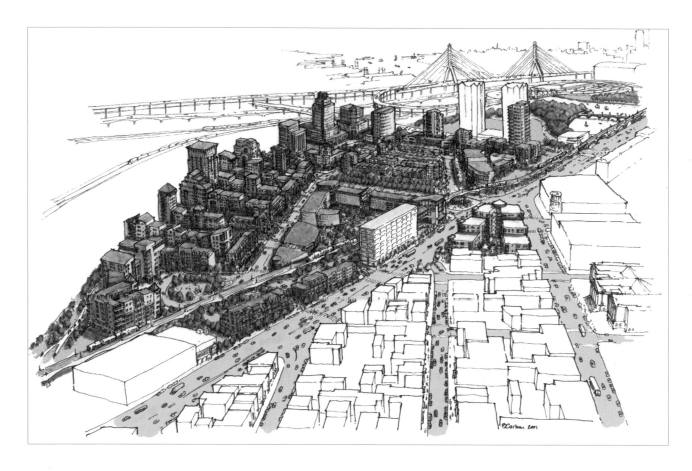

The plan for NorthPoint, in Cambridge, Massachusetts, incorporates higher-density mixed-use structures without overwhelming the pedestrian scale of the surrounding neighborhood.

Graphic: Goody Clancy

encourages such enticements for venturing further in the urban experience. Design solutions for mixed-use developments can challenge urban designers' capabilities for creating exciting places while ensuring economic sustainability and mitigating the potentially incompatible qualities of a project's components.

The story of the strategic plan for the neighborhood of East Cambridge, in Cambridge, Massachusetts, shows how neighborhoods in transition have accepted greater diversity as a means of enhancing the living environment. Sustained economic growth in the area had increased development pressures to the point that citizens petitioned for and won an 18-month moratorium on further development. They pushed for this moratorium to allow time for the preparation of a growth strategy plan by an 18-member committee working with consultants Goody Clancy, a Boston planning and design firm.

At the time, East Cambridge was made up of historic, mixed-income, tightly knit neighborhoods (mostly traditional one- and two-family homes) and a mix of commercial and office buildings. At the northern end was a large open area that was available for development. Discussions revealed a concern that new commercial buildings would overshadow the pedestrian-scale neighborhood environment, community-oriented shops and services, and local parks. The committee gradually developed a strategy that leveraged designs for new development that would enhance rather than degrade adjoining neighborhoods. The plan created a new mixed-use district with strong visual and pedestrian connections among the neighborhoods, a sizeable new park, additional affordable housing, and limits on heights of new buildings from three stories next to traditional residential areas to 25 or more stories next to transit stations. The committee approved 7.3 million square feet (680,000 sq m) of new construction, including about 4,400 new residential units. Within months developers submitted proposals for a substantial amount of development to be based on the committee's plans.

The Crossings at Gresham Station in Gresham, Oregon, is an affordable housing development clustered around transit.

Photo: Myhre Group

EXPANDING LIFESTYLE CHOICES

Urban design models that advance density and diversity encourage development that makes available a range of lifestyle options—a variety of housing, employment, living, recreational, and cultural environments. Across metropolitan regions, real urbanism provides for a spectrum of lifestyles that embrace density and diversity as well as quiet.

Inspired design should not be reserved only for wealthy residents and upscale neighborhoods; it must meet the requirements of lower-income households and neighborhoods as well. Urban designs and development plans can promote the economic vitality that spurs job creation in both existing and developing neighborhoods. A good plan can put new homes near jobs and can make jobs more accessible by transit. Such plans can provide for recreational and cultural activities. They can place homes close enough to schools for children to walk or bike, and they can establish schools as a focal point of neighborhood activity. A plan that considers pedestrian movement, in terms of scale, access, and amenities, can also make walking an option for daily shopping and service destinations.

The transformation of the Pearl District in Portland, Oregon, epitomizes the range of lifestyles that truly urban areas can accommodate. During the mid–20th century, much of this former transportation hub and manufacturing and warehouse district had been abandoned and its previous activities marginalized, despite its advantageous location bordering downtown Portland, the I-405 highway, and the Willamette River. But in the late 1970s, artists began moving into the roomy, inexpensive warehouses, creating loft dwellings and galleries, sparking a resurgence of interest in the centrally located area. Soon the Pearl District was attracting restaurants, nightspots, and shops that have made it an increasingly lively social draw. By the 1990s, developers saw opportunities for redevelopment, with Hoyt Street Properties acquiring the 34-acre (13.8-ha) Burlington Northern railyard in 1994 and initiating a massive mixed-use housing project that attracted considerable attention. A second project by Gerding/Edlen Development Company began in 2000 to adapt the five-block cluster of historic buildings of the Blitz-Weinhard Brewery for more housing and retail uses.

In the meantime, the city's River District Urban Renewal Plan, which included the establishment of a tax increment financing program, has guided key public investments. Public efforts have focused on completion of the Portland streetcar line, linking the area directly to downtown and the northwest neighborhoods; improving streetscapes; and planning a series of four new parks—the first one being Jamison Square in the district's center, noted for its cascading water feature for children. The city also has ensured the creation of hundreds of affordable housing units, as a significant contribution to the residential boom that has regenerated the neighborhood. By 2020, the district is expected to grow by another 10,000 residents and add a similar number of jobs.[4]

Portland's enterprising ways have restored a historic, architecturally rich part of the city, fashioning an exciting environment that appeals to the so-called creative class, as well as offering homes for disadvantaged households near vital services and transportation lines. The district is an artful mix of housing and an enticing night-and-day destination for visitors from near and far, making it an economic boon for the city.

MULTIMODAL TRANSPORTATION

It is no secret that Americans love cars and that most American households are highly dependent on them; typically, an American's longest walk is from a parking space to a shopping mall. Cars are ever present in the landscape and fill huge surface parking areas and garages. At homes they are often awarded spaces larger than the master bedroom. But truly urban places are not car-friendly. Density and diversity cause

problems for drivers—generating congestion that necessitates searching for parking places; keeping an eye on traffic, pedestrians, and bikers; and often warily surrendering the car to parking attendants.

Such inconveniences help make other forms of travel attractive in urban communities, at least for some proportion of daily trips. That is why the true vitality of any urban setting is revealed on its sidewalks, where walkability is king and pedestrians can see and be seen, can stroll and window-shop, can run errands and meet acquaintances. Pedestrian

Del Mar Station was key
to revitalizing downtown
Pasadena.

Photo: Moule & Polyzoides

activity flourishes when people live near services and their work, and
when they can benefit from efficient public transit that delivers them
close to their destinations. Walkability requires interesting destinations
that draw people to them, with buildings close to the sidewalks. It also
requires that destinations be interconnected by a continuous network
of safe, convenient, attractive sidewalks and paths.

Public transit systems are most successful in densely built older cities.
Today, new and improved transit systems in many cities, such as Dallas
and Denver, are gaining ridership in part because regionwide traffic congestion has become so onerous. Greater use of rail transit, in particular,
has generated interest in development around transit stations that
attempts to replicate the pedestrian-friendly neighborhoods and generate the street life of older cities. Portland's Pearl District and the Bethesda
Row project provide examples of fairly dense, diverse development that
has occurred hand in hand with transit improvements.

Pasadena, California's experience in promoting transit-oriented development around its downtown Del Mar station highlights a number of
favorable factors. First, Pasadena had a history of building along the

Atchison-Topeka and Santa Fe Railway lines. While the 13.7-mile (22-km) Gold Line was being extended from downtown Los Angeles to Pasadena, the city planned for station-area development of an urban village with a mix of uses and housing types, in a pedestrian-oriented environment. Subsequent development reflected the benefits of early planning and effective local policies, the availability of development subsidies and opportunities for land assembly, and the participation of knowledgeable developers who took advantage of favorable market conditions. Several developments opened in advance of the Gold Line's startup date of 2003. The Del Mar Station project, for example, comprises 374 apartments in four buildings; shops and restaurants occupy the fully restored Santa Fe Railroad Depot, and a 1,210-car underground parking facility reserves 600 spaces for transit users. Walkability is a central element, and public courtyards and plazas provide views to design features that reflect the city's rich Spanish, art deco, Craftsman, and modern architectural heritage.[5]

It is instructive, however, that the transit-oriented developments of both Bethesda Row and Del Mar Station incorporate substantial parking

The Del Mar Station project in Pasadena, California, offers housing, retail, and restaurant options clustered around a light-rail station. The architectural elements draw from local themes.

Photo: Moule & Polyzoides

Parking garages in Midtown Miami, Florida, were designed to resemble other structures and keep cars out of view, making a pedestrian-friendly streetscape.

Photo: Steven Brooke

facilities, working from the premise that many residents, shoppers, transit users, and other visitors will arrive and depart by car. (Residents and visitors in Portland's Pearl District, adjacent to downtown, are less dependent on cars, although parking space is still at a premium.) Moreover, transit services are limited in many metropolitan regions—particularly in the south and west—that grew up in the automobile-centric, post–World War II era. Although most urban areas offer at least minimal bus services and a growing number of cities offer light-rail service as well, only a relatively small number offer a full range of transit modes including rapid-transit or commuter-rail services. It is important to note that ridership most often increases once more localized neighborhood transit networks are in place to help get riders from their neighborhoods to the main transit lines.

Even in urban settings, however, personal vehicles remain the most common form of transportation, requiring efficient street networks and adequate parking as critical elements for commerce, livability, and recreation. The close-knit street grid typical of older cities has proven highly adaptable to these needs, offering many route options and often allowing on-street parking.

Streets can be designed to respect and support urban conditions with the following guidelines:

- Enhance the appearance of streets by using special paving, street furniture, and integrated plantings.
- Design streets for safe use by using traffic calming devices and paving widths that are adequate but not excessive for expected traffic.
- Provide pathways for bikes and pedestrians either along the street or in separate rights-of-way.
- Relate street designs to the natural and historical setting, including terrain, plantings, and details such as curb design, sidewalk paving, and street signs.

Including off-street parking to serve urban centers is often an urban designer's nightmare, with images of cars squeezed hither and thither into leftover spaces among the buildings, creating unsightly car-scapes for blocks. Often, structured parking is not much better: bare-bones façades expose parked cars looming high over sidewalks; dingy entrances interrupt street life, in contrast to the lively shops and offices they serve. Thoughtful designers consider parking structures

The Mirador parking garage in South Beach, Florida, is designed with residential liner units, which serve to integrate it into the scale and pattern of the street plan, and to obscure the cars from the view of passersby.

Photo: Zyscovich

as significant elements of urban life and plan accordingly. For example, they create structures lined with street-level shops and upper-level residential frontages. These wrapped buildings hide the garages and add more life to the streets, enhancing the pedestrian experience and improving safety.

EFFICIENT INFRASTRUCTURE AND PUBLIC SERVICES

In addition to transportation facilities, other infrastructure systems and public services play key roles in urban design. For example, development in older parts of cities may require expensive upgrading or rebuilding of deteriorating water, wastewater, and drainage systems. Designs for new development may incorporate innovative "green" techniques that reduce reliance on existing systems, such as water-absorbing green roofs or graywater facilities, as described in chapter 3. Civic facilities, particularly schools and libraries that directly serve neighborhood residents, are primary elements for creating a sense of community. Such neighborhood-oriented facilities provide opportunities to bring together children and parents of diverse economic and cultural backgrounds, exposing residents to various traditions. Neighborhood schools thus provide a means of generating familiarity, supporting friendships, and strengthening the livability of neighborhoods. In addition, schools and libraries often provide facilities for other neighborhood services and activities, such as health screenings, political organizing, and community meetings and hearings.

In undertaking redevelopment projects for affordable housing across the nation, developer Richard Baron of McCormack, Baron, Salazar places great value on improving local schools. In 1996, when Baron began the planning efforts for redeveloping a public housing project in St. Louis into a mixed-income project, the school situation was abysmal. At the time, owing to gang warfare and drug dealing around the local school, the neighborhood children were sent to more than 25 schools across the city. Baron worked with the local board of education to revamp the nearby Jefferson Elementary School as a neighborhood school and raised $3.5 million in contributions from 20 corporations, to improve the building and sponsor teacher training and special student programs. Now, 70 percent of the schoolchildren in the Murphy Park development live within walking distance of their schools, and the Jefferson school has become a busy center of activity for the neighborhood. In other cities as well, Baron has made a practice of planning for neighborhood schools as mainstays of his neighborhood redevelopment programs.

Opposite: Miami Senior High School in Miami, Florida, has been restored to its Mediterranean Revival–style glory, serving not only as an educational facility but as the focus of community life and a center of civic resources.

Graphic: Zyscovich

Another example: Miami Senior High School, built in 1927, is listed on the National Register of Historic Places. Having fallen into a state of serious disrepair, the once beautiful Mediterranean Revival–style school is being renovated and modernized, beginning with a master plan prepared by Zyscovich Architects.

Originally designed for the subtropical climate, the school has double-loaded classroom wings separated by four parallel courtyards, which introduced both fresh air and daylight into the classrooms. Cast-stone vent panels high on the walls between the classrooms and hallways

ensured cross-ventilation through the buildings. Roofed arcades provided protection from sun and rain. The exterior featured elaborate cast-stone work in an incredible variety of forms: portals, window frames, columns, railings, vents, and cornice moldings, among others. In addition, the siting of the school was masterful—set back one block from Flagler Street (once Miami's main east-west street) across a green block which eventually became known as Columbia Park.

On a central axis between rows of royal palms is the commanding four-story central structure with three decorative cast-stone entry portals. The original heavy oak doors are still in place, protected in their deep recesses. Above are two stories of tall, slender, arched windows, capped on the fourth floor by a smaller suite that was originally the music recital space. The name of the school (in gothic script) is incorporated into the cast-stone parapet between the third and fourth floors.

The richly detailed auditorium is the most spectacular space, needing only cosmetic repairs and replacement of the 1,100 seats. The original library and study hall, which will be restored and expanded into a state-of-the-art media center, has decorative steel trusses with unique spiral scrollwork that was hidden for years behind acoustical ceiling tiles.

Modifications made over the years will be corrected in the historically faithful rehabilitation. Most significantly, when the school was air-conditioned in the mid-1960s, the delicate, steel-framed, projecting windows were almost all replaced by infilled walls and minimal windows. New hurricane-impact windows with configurations similar to the original designs will be installed. Poorly designed additions will be removed to reveal the original building and landscaping. To create space for more students and reduce class sizes, three new buildings will be added. They will also provide enough space to allow phased restoration of the existing building.

The relationship between the high school and its urban neighborhood is important, and the renovation is helping to make the facility more available to the community. The gym, auditorium, cafeteria, and dining courtyard will all be used for cultural performances and community events. The original home economics living room, complete with an ornamented fireplace, custom millwork, and original local pine flooring, is being restored as the Miami High historic museum. Here, copies of historic photos and artifacts will be on display to visitors who wish to tour the premises.

Community involvement has been an important aspect of the renovation. Howard Kleinberg, former publisher of the *Miami News* and school alumni association president, helped orient the design team to the rich history of the school. A group of alumni came forward to identify ways they could support the renovation and the enrichment of the school and students after the project is complete. Finally, local historic preservation activists have advocated the project to the school board, which is very important in a period of tightening public funding.

Both the St. Louis and Miami examples indicate the importance of schools as civic resources in neighborhoods and communities. They furnish space for community as well as educational activities and frequently contribute to the neighborhoods' distinctive identity.

DISTINCTIVE COMMUNITIES

People like communities with memorable qualities. In *The Ecology of Place*, Timothy Beatley and Kristy Manning maintain that cities and towns worth caring about possess "a strong and appealing local identity, an ambiance of belonging, and a sense of place."[6] Such a sense,

they suggest, comes from feelings of connection to the history or the landscape or the built environment of the community. Residents and visitors identify with the place, and that feeling gives them comfort and promotes their interest in the well-being of the place.

Healthy cities facilitate human interaction through good design. It is not about buildings alone, says ULI senior fellow William Hudnut: "It's about the public realm, the parks and plazas, boulevards and streets, squares and fountains and open spaces, libraries, post offices, community centers, and places of worship." The value of such places comes in part in reaction to the omnipresence of suburban strip malls and acres of all-alike houses around so many cities and towns. People have grown bored with the monotony of so much recent development and prefer to look instead to more distinctive urban environments, real places with distinguishing features and spaces for gathering and hobnobbing. The current popularity of lifestyle retail centers, which encourage leisurely strolling and relaxation among colorfully designed storefronts and landscaped settings, reflects this interest. Many such centers add residential and office uses on upper floors or adjacent to the retail frontage to enhance their place-making qualities. Hudnut points to the renovations of more than 6,000 main streets being carried out across the nation, as well as the hundreds of new town centers being created by developers, as testimony to the strength of place making as a means of creating community identity.

A district of downtown San Francisco was brought back to life by the renovation of a building and the surrounding plaza. The 1898 beaux arts Ferry Building on San Francisco's waterfront was a treasured landmark for generations of residents and visitors alike. The building's distinctive tower marked the primary point of arrival and departure for downtown until the Golden Gate and Bay bridges opened in the late 1930s. The cherished status of the building encouraged city officials to embark on a major rehabilitation of the structure in 2003, attracting new uses that would reenergize the waterfront's activities and revitalize its economic strength. Now 65,000 square feet (6,000 sq m) of ground-floor space is occupied by cafés, shops, and restaurants and a popular organic farmers market, whose activity spills out onto the plaza. The second and third floors provide 175,000 square feet (16,000 sq m) of Class A office space, the revenues from which help support the public market. Robert Winter, executive vice president for the principal investor, Equity Office Properties Trust, says, "The completion of the Ferry Building rehabilitation restores the landmark to its historic role as a bustling transportation hub and an elegant centerpiece of the waterfront." The project won an Urban Land Institute award in 2004.[7]

Another kind of place making is occurring in downtown Burlington, Iowa, where Downtown Partners, Inc. (DPI), a community-based development organization, has worked to revitalize the city's commercial core through the Main Street program of the National Trust for Historic Preservation. DPI has promoted the rehabilitation of many downtown buildings, including the nine-story Hotel Burlington, which now provides affordable housing for senior citizens, and the Old Stone Mill, which has

Opposite: The rehabilitated Ferry Building draws tourists, residents, and workers from nearby offices to its shops and restaurants.

Photo: Equity Office

been transformed into an antiques mall. DPI also runs a business incubator and plans events to keep downtown lively, with activities that range from a weekly farmers market to the annual Snake Alley Criterium bicycle race.

Both San Francisco and Burlington have benefited from reinforcing the sense of place in their communities, a quality that builds *communitas*, togetherness, and identity.

URBAN PARKS AND SQUARES

Cities and towns should regard the conservation of natural landscapes as no less important for sustaining urban life than the construction of transportation, water supply systems, schools, and other public facilities and amenities. Green spaces—parks, playgrounds, waterfronts, and gardens, for example—support the urban quality of life that inhabitants value and the natural environment on which all people depend. Even as we build urban domains, planners must seek ways to retain nature's functions. Ideally, nature's green spaces and features are best conserved as strategically planned, interconnected networks—especially those nestled within and around built-up areas. Such a vision presents a powerful means of enriching community design and development.

Ian McHarg, in his classic book *Design with Nature*, teaches the reader to think of green spaces as natural life-support systems—ecosystems made up of waterways, wetlands, woodlands, wildlife habitats, greenways, parks, and recreation areas, all helping support a pleasurable living environment for city dwellers, whether animal, vegetable, or human. Parks, recreation areas, and nature preserves offer welcome breathing spaces in busy urban environments, and even formal, landscaped urban squares offer greenery and sunlight. Greenways and trails lead through and to nature's wonders. Not only parks and playgrounds

The South Bank Redevelopment Project provided 42 acres (17 ha) of public open space in the center of Brisbane—Australia's fastest-growing city.

Photo: South Bank Corporation

but also home gardens and larger community gardens provide healthful recreational opportunities. These benefits convey positive images to community residents, workers, and visitors; perceptions of welcoming green spaces stick in people's minds.

The value of green spaces as essential elements of even the most dense urban development has long been acknowledged. The positive effect of New York's Central Park on property values around it is legendary, and the success of the rejuvenated Bryant Park in 1992, in midtown Manhattan, proved the worth of a lively yet relaxing green space. Chicago's expansive Lake Michigan waterfront and linear park and its newest addition, Millennium Park, demonstrate the image-making strength and popular magnetism of green spaces in urban areas. Boston's Emerald Necklace of beautiful parks and Washington, D.C.'s Rock Creek Park, which extends

The Sabine-to-Bagby Promenade in Houston, Texas, replaced a trash-strewn waterfront as a 3,000-foot (914-m) linear park acting as a signature gateway to downtown.

Photo: Tom Fox

from the Potomac River into neighboring counties, all create living, natural corridors of major ecological value to the regions. Pittsburgh's former mayor Tom Murphy observes that greenways and trails have been a significant factor in revitalizing his city's riverfront area, once a scene of industrial blight and abandonment.

Planners in Bellevue, Washington, a first-tier suburb of Seattle, looked to the development of a new central park as an important image maker for the city. Locally regarded as a rather bland suburban community,

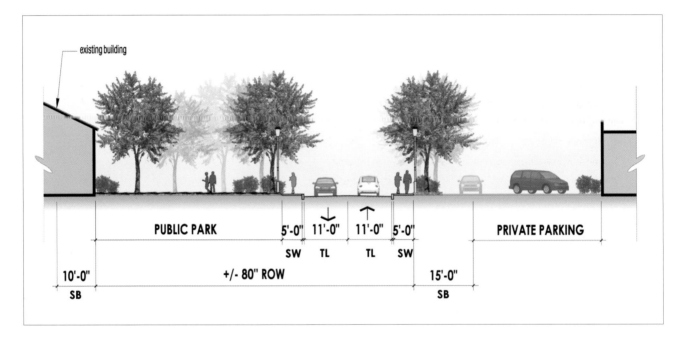

Bellevue had succeeded in attracting a considerable amount of downtown development. City officials aspired to create a signature park that would establish downtown as a distinctly urban place. Designed as a rather formal, elegant space, with a strong European influence, the park succeeded in drawing attention and also generated significant new residential development nearby.

Urban parks need not be green oases; many are composed of ornamental pavements rather than grass or plantings. Urban squares in European cities such as Siena and Prague come quickly to mind, but American cities such as Portland and Boise boast paved open spaces as well. The central element in Portland's Jamison Square park, completed in 2002, is a multilevel stone wall from which water cascades to fill a shallow semicircular basin. Once the basin fills, the water recedes into the base of the stone wall, then flows again, always gentle and shallow enough for toddlers to splash in. The fountain and park offer many options for enjoyment. The wall's levels are suitable for climbing and sitting, and the water cascading down the levels leaves some climbers and sitters dry and some soaked. When the fountain is flowing, the paved plaza becomes a beach, beyond which a semicircle of grass allows more relaxed—and drier—play. When the fountain is turned off, the basin becomes a shallow amphitheater. The park's multiuse and practical design features have made it very popular with local residents.

Developers of urban projects also understand the place-making value of green spaces in attracting shoppers and residents. Market Common Clarendon, a mixed-use development in Arlington, Virginia, is developed on just over 14 acres (6 ha) along both sides of a major through street about a block from a Metrorail station. Through skillful design it packs 303,000 square feet (28,000 sq m) of retail space, 101,000 square feet (9,000 sq m) of office space, 87 townhouses, and 300 rental apartment units, plus 1,100 parking spaces, on three compact parcels. The designers also found room for an elongated landscaped courtyard, around which the shops and restaurants are clustered, and added three small parks oriented to the residential buildings. The green spaces and appealing streetscapes provide inviting, safe, and interesting outdoor experiences for residents, visitors, and shoppers alike.

Another form of green space that has gained considerable popularity in urban areas is the greenway or trail, which may meander through natural areas but frequently passes through built environments. Often these trails make use of abandoned railroad rights-of-way. Seattle's 18-mile (29-km) Burke-Gilman Trail, which passes through the University of Washington's campus and along the shoreline of Lake Washington before joining the Sammamish River Trail for 15 more miles (24 km), is a favored route for students, commuters, and hikers.

The Capital Crescent Trail in the Washington, D.C., area follows a former railway route that originated in historic Georgetown and crosses through the Bethesda Row development to intersect with other trails in Montgomery County. Heavily used by bikers and hikers, the trail is bordered by wooded areas for much of its distance but offers glimpses of its urban setting.

In Minneapolis, the Midtown Greenway is a 5.5-mile-long (8.9-km) biking and walking trail on a former railroad bed. Though most of its distance, the trail is grade-separated from streets, offering safe, barrier-free biking and hiking. The Greenway connects with other regional pathways, allowing users to travel considerable distances on bike or foot. The popular trail is lit for night use and draws thousands of users daily throughout much of the year. Eventually, the trail will be accessible by rail transit.

Opposite: Linear parks, like this one proposed for Atlantic Beach, South Carolina, improve the pedestrian environment and help slow traffic.

Graphic: Zyscovich

These greenways link parks, playing fields, and other green spaces and establish city- or regionwide green infrastructure systems. In these ways, green spaces provide breathing room for urban residents and workers and, with careful consideration, can be designed to conserve and improve important environmental assets, including air and water quality, as described further in chapter 3.

EFFECTIVE, COLLABORATIVE DECISION MAKING

Fair, predictable, and cost-effective development decisions based on community involvement and collaboration are essential to promoting urban revitalization. Real urban places require an understanding of the

evolving nature of the built environment and an appreciation of the current concerns of residents, property owners, and other interests about its future course. The days when public officials framed development policies and projects, heedless of these concerns, are past. People involved in an area proposed for development or revitalization expect to be consulted about plans and designs. In the planning programs for the FEC and East Cambridge projects, for example, multiple discussions with local leaders and residents fed information and ideas into the design process, influencing such matters as appropriate densities and relationships among various uses. Chapter 5 details the purposes and procedures for such consultations.

The Market Common Clarendon in Arlington, Virginia, is an infill development designed to knit together a previously declining urban district. It creates green space in an elongated courtyard and is within a short walk of a subway station.

Photo: Sisson Studios

Applying the Guiding Principles

These principles for guiding the design of urban development are applicable across the spectrum of urban conditions, although their relative significance may vary according to the character of the area. For example, when built-up districts become increasingly attractive for additional growth, they may present planning and design opportunities that are unlikely to arise in distressed or stagnant neighborhoods. Possibilities for the development of overlooked and underdeveloped properties can pose different issues than similar situations in commercial centers that are ripe for revitalization and renewal. The scale of the prospective development, market strength, sources of financial and community support, and other factors play a part in determining the degree to which designers can reflect the principles in plans for development.

Targeted public and private investments have helped to revitalize downtown Arlington Heights, Illinois, an older, first-tier suburb of Chicago.

Photo: Village of
Arlington Heights

For example, areas where strong markets favor more intensive development are likely to attract private developers who can easily find financial partners. But the developers may require regulatory changes or special permissions to achieve the mix and density of uses most appropriate for available sites. At the same time, past public actions may have heightened market interest in the area, which may prompt public agencies to request developers' contributions to community needs for affordable housing, civic improvements, or cultural facilities. The development process in Portland's Pearl District exemplifies circumstances in which public investments in center-city redevelopment and transportation infrastructure helped generate a burgeoning market for in-city living. As a result of those investments, developers initiated substantial residential and mixed-use projects in the district. The combination of public and private efforts is creating a distinctive sector of central Portland and

achieving city goals for revitalizing a former industrial area and expanding the stock of affordable housing. In return, property owners and
developers in the Pearl District are benefiting from the city's eagerness
to approve major projects, complete a streetcar line, improve
streetscapes, and invest in new parks that add to the district's ambience and appeal.

However, revitalization of a moribund neighborhood or commercial
center frequently requires significant long-term investments by public
agencies. The Village of Arlington Heights, Illinois, first settled in the
1830s, became a city of 77,000 residents as one of the Chicago area's
commuter hubs. But its substantial downtown withered as shopping
malls proliferated on its fringe during the 1960s and 1970s. Buildings
were torn down to make room for parking lots and others stood vacant;

few active businesses remained. The village council fought back, hoping to attract redevelopment by establishing a tax increment financing district in 1983 and adopting a master plan for the central business district four years later. Subsequently, the village invested in the construction of parking garages, new parks, and improved streetscapes.

Arlington Heights began reaping the rewards of its long battle to rescue its town center in 1999, with the development of an in-town, mixed-use town center on a site owned by a public/private partnership consisting of the village and the developer. Construction of three condominium buildings and a performing arts center in the next two years added about 850 residential units to the downtown. With the village creating a town square park and additional residential growth planned for the future, downtown Arlington Heights has been revitalized. After 30 years of planning, targeted public investments, and inspired public/private cooperation, the village offers residents a walkable, attractive, thriving downtown.

Conclusion

Guiding principles for creating urbanism are just that—guides or leads to designing elements of cities that can provide workable and enjoyable urban environments. The guiding principles here offer directions that must be interpreted for the particular time and place at hand, as well as the goals to be achieved. They afford opportunities for creative, innovative forms and functions of urban development. Rising interest in and concerns about promoting sustainable, green development add significant perspectives to the guiding principles. Most important, designers should understand that the principles apply within specific urban contexts that influence the design outcome.

Opposite: Careful planning has resulted in the revitalization of Arlington Heights, Illinois.

Photo: Village of Arlington Heights

1 Based in part on the principles listed by the Smart Growth Leadership Institute, "Smart Growth Quick Diagnostic," p. ii, in *Smart Growth Implementation Toolkit*, December 2007, www.smartgrowthtoolkit.net.

2 See William P. Macht, "Outgoing Infill," *Urban Land*, August 2004, pp. 28–29.

3 Roberta Brandes Gratz, *Cities Back from the Edge* (New York: John Wiley & Sons, Inc., 2000), p. 344.

4 Information drawn from www.explorethepearl.com, www.hoytstreetproperties.com, www.pdc.us/ura, www.nextbus.com, and Mark Hinshaw, "True Urbanism," *Planning*, June 2005, p. 27.

5 The description of the Del Mar Station project is drawn from Maureen McAvey, "Urban Opportunities," in Robert T. Dunphy, et al., *Developing Around Transit: Strategies and Solutions That Work* (Washington, D.C.: Urban Land Institute, 2004), p. 103.

6 Timothy Beatley and Kristy Manning, *The Ecology of Place* (Washington, D.C.: Island Press, 1997), p. 175.

7 David Takesuye, *ULI Awards for Excellence* (Washington, D.C.: Urban Land Institute, 2004), pp. 12–13.

"SUSTAINABLE" AND "GREEN" have become watchwords for urban designers, who tend to use the terms rather interchangeably to express their concerns about the effects of development on the local and global environment. And there is reason to worry: buildings account for the largest source of energy consumption in America and emit about 43 percent of all greenhouse gases, compared with 32 percent from transportation and 25 percent from industry.[1] Buildings

3   sustainable, green urbanism

squander more energy than even cars or trucks. The tremendous growth of the world's population and the associated declines in biodiversity and air and water quality also add to concerns about the scale and character of urban development.

The Brookings Institution projects that half the buildings that Americans will live in by 2030 have yet to be constructed.[2] This suggests that opportunities for addressing these issues in future development will be plentiful. Jenifer Seal Cramer, editor of the spring 2007 issue of *Urban Land Green*, points this out:

> The building industry will need not only to supply new developments to meet these growing demands, but also to work on transforming the existing fabric of communities into life-enriching developments, while reducing dependence on fossil fuels, producing a zero-carbon footprint, and restoring lost landscapes.[3]

Many mayors apparently agree. In June 2006 the U.S. Conference of Mayors voted to commit member cities to reducing the negative environmental impacts of buildings by reducing allowable greenhouse gas emissions from new and renovated buildings by 50 percent and requiring new buildings to be carbon neutral by 2030.[4]

The guiding spirit of sustainable development was defined in the 1987 report of the Brundtland Commission, an international group sponsored by the United Nations:

> development that integrates environmental, economic, and social concerns that can meet the needs of the present without compromising the ability of future generations to meet their own needs.[5]

In the broadest sense, sustainable development presents an all-encompassing goal of keeping the world and its inhabitants alive and well indefinitely. For urban designers, this means moving beyond the core principles of urbanism described in chapter 2 to create structures and places for human activities that respect the interests of future generations. That

Mixed-use buildings on Main Street in the New Columbia development in Portland, Oregon, attained the U.S. Green Building Council's LEED certification. The landscaping in the project reduces heat islands, and 98 percent of stormwater is retained on the site. So-called "skinny streets" minimize paved surface area, helping to limit runoff.

Photo: Pete Eckert

is a tall order. It requires new ways of thinking about designing buildings and development projects while maintaining the integrity of natural features and qualities. Ultimately, sustainable development requires designers to pay attention to the social and economic effects of their products. This chapter probes the manner in which designers can instill green, sustainable qualities in developments that are conceived to achieve the principles of urbanism.

Thinking Green

Designers were introduced to the concept of sustainability through long exposure to the benefits of conserving natural areas. Decades ago, prompted by new environmental laws, designers learned to respect green features of development sites. Many take to heart Frederick Law Olmsted's regard for preservation of green space and Ian McHarg's techniques for landscape evaluation, and routinely factor ecosystem concerns into their plans and designs. Many admirable plans and designs for development, especially in suburban greenfield areas, carefully skirt wetlands and wildlife habitats and preserve hillsides and stream valleys.

Planners of large-scale communities routinely retain swaths of green landscapes to preserve natural features and, not incidentally, to provide valued amenities for residents. Even relatively small-scale developments, such as the 226-acre (92-ha) The Fields of St. Croix in Lake Elmo, Minnesota, call for homes on rather small lots in order to set aside conserved natural areas for farming, woodlands, and parklands for the enjoyment of residents. The 39-acre (16-ha) Prairie Glen project in

Opposite: Green urbanism takes many forms, from lily ponds to sustainable high-rises. Pictured here is the Solaire, the first LEED Gold residential building in the United States, rising behind Battery Park in New York City.

Photo: Battery Park City Authority

Above: Battery Park in New York's lower Manhattan features a landscaped esplanade highlighting dramatic waterfront views.

Photo: Stan Ries Photography

Left: The city of Vancouver, Canada, is a haven for urban hiking, biking, sunning, and strolling. Its linear park runs along much of the city's coastline, linking neighborhoods with beaches and marinas.

Photo: Adrienne Schmitz

In Seattle, Washington, Harbor Steps is a mixed-use infill development of four high-rise towers that contributes to the urban vitality of the neighborhood. The paved open space, dominated by a series of cascading fountains, forms an inviting pedestrian link between the lively downtown street and the waterfront below.

Photo: Adrienne Schmitz

Germantown, Wisconsin, restored partially degraded wetlands to act as a stormwater treatment system. Through these types of approaches, many designers have acquired a considerable amount of experience in preserving green space within suburban developments.

In built-up urban areas, however, designers rely to a great extent on the legacy of public parks and expansive green landscapes established a century or more ago, such as Central Park in New York City, the Emerald Necklace of Boston, and Rock Creek Park in Washington, D.C. Cities along the east and west coasts have set aside beaches and coastal areas as public spaces. With the abandonment of industrial areas along riverbanks in the mid–20th century, cities have rediscovered urban waterfronts as highly desirable green space. Waterfronts often support other green values, in the form of extensive habitats for wildlife and floodplains that absorb potentially destructive stormwater.

Residents of many cities and towns now have access to rejuvenated waterfronts for recreational use. For example, Charleston, South Carolina's Waterfront Park on the Cooper River was redesigned to create a place of natural beauty that would serve as a counterpoint to the city's dense downtown area. As Charleston mayor Joseph Riley, Jr., noted at the park's opening ceremony in 1990, "This is to be a quiet park. . .a place of repose along the water's edge for all citizens to enjoy."[6]

The design favored intimate seating areas, walking paths, and pleasant gardens, all conducive to strolling, jogging, fishing, or just relaxing. Cincinnati embraced opportunities for extending access to the Ohio River, constructing two new ballparks and the National Underground Railroad Freedom Center on the city's waterfront. In Louisville, Kentucky, the popular 85-acre (34.4-ha) Waterfront Park draws more than

Left and below: Waterfront Park in Louisville, Kentucky, averages more than 1.5 million visitors per year and includes numerous lawns, walking paths, and fountains.

Photos: Waterfront Development Corporation

1.5 million people each year from around the region for recreation and entertainment, galvanizing major development on the waterfront and transforming the image of Louisville. Pittsburgh and San Diego are working on expanding green spaces along their waterfronts.

Much of Chicago's reputation as a green-minded city stems from its care for and improvement of the city's 20-mile (32-km) waterfront along Lake Michigan, a product of deliberate planning and design decisions made a century ago and cultivated ever since. The city's lakefront now boasts clean water and sandy beaches, miles of playing fields, magnificent gardens, impressive museums, and an extensive network of interconnected lakefront bike and walking trails. But the city has done much more to win acclaim for going green. Since the 1990s, it has poured millions of dollars into upgrading city parks, converting asphalt schoolyards to grassy playgrounds, and turning vacant, tax-delinquent private lots into community gardens. The city has created greenways and wildlife habitats along inland waterways, plants 30,000 new trees a year, and tends to 70 miles (113 km) of green medians in city streets. City regulations now require gardens and other green spaces for all new homes, stores, and office buildings. Mayor Daly's crowning achievement is the design and construction of Millennium Park, a 24.5-acre (9.9-ha) urban park built over an underground parking garage. Most noted for its Frank Gehry–designed concert pavilion, the park also features an ice rink, significant sculptures, landscaped areas, a wild-grass prairie, and gardens. It replaces a huge railroad yard that separated the South Loop from the lakeshore. The park is an effective bridge, both aesthetically and functionally, between the urban core and the waterfront.

Cities demand another form of conservation—that of the urban structure itself, including the buildings in which people live and work and the infrastructure systems that support their functions. The objective of greening cities must give high priority to reusing, rebuilding, and improving structures and, when required, replacing deteriorated structures with greener ones. Increasingly, designers are seizing opportunities for conserving urban buildings and in-city areas—in effect, acting to renew cityscapes in addition to landscapes. Over time, they have acquired knowledge and experience in redevelopment of once-contaminated brownfield sites and revitalizing underused or obsolete areas.

Summerset, an infill residential development in Pittsburgh, provides an excellent example of a triumph over substantial environmental disincentives for development. The residential project is in the final stages of building 240 upscale homes on a huge slag heap, a legacy of the city's once-thriving steel industry. The remediation of the pile of slag and

Opposite: The recent development of Millennium Park on downtown Chicago's lake shore created a vibrant, active-use park that includes performance venues, a skating rink, and an assortment of sculptural and landscaping elements, while below the surface, commuters are still served by trains and a 4,000-car garage. Pictured: Cloud Gate, a stainless steel sculpture that reflects its surroundings.

Photo: Joe-Urban.com

restoration of the stream running through the property serves Summerset residents and Pittsburgh citizens alike. Residents enjoy the wonderful river views and landscaped trails leading down to the Monongahela River. They also value access to the city's largest green space, venerable Frick Park, as well as the project's central location near downtown and the university area. The city, of course, benefits from the addition of new residents moving to the city's once-declining neighborhood.

There is much yet to accomplish. The U.S. Environmental Protection Agency reports that in the United States, buildings account for 68 percent of electricity consumption, 39 percent of energy use, 38 percent of carbon dioxide emissions, and 12 percent of water consumption. In the early years of this century, urban designers took a giant step toward grappling with these and other fundamental issues of sustainability—"going green," as some say. Advances in technology paved the way for designers to consider alternatives to standard building technologies that greatly enhance energy efficiency, conserve building materials, safeguard water resources, and improve indoor air quality. Today, green building has become an important objective for designers, particularly for development in dense urban areas.

Some experts claim that reducing the energy consumption of buildings may be the single most important factor in creating sustainable buildings, in part because energy is used in so many forms and stages of building construction and management—in acquiring, manufacturing, and transporting the materials of construction; in preparing the site and assembling the structure; in disposing of waste; and finally in managing a building's internal heating, cooling, lighting, and other systems.

Technology and the designers and builders who use it have gone far beyond the solar panels and high-performance glass that constituted the initial step toward improving energy efficiency. A glimpse of some of the technologies now being used can be seen in the Four Times Square Building in New York City, one of the first commercial towers to incorporate a wide range of energy-saving features. After evaluating the variety of possibilities, its designers chose large windows that provide daylighting but minimize solar heat gain, electrical generation using fuel cells and photovoltaic cells, use of natural gas as the cleanest-burning fossil fuel, and an energy-efficient absorption chiller for air conditioning.

Another recent project in Manhattan, the 46-story Hearst Tower designed by Lord Norman Foster, opened in 2006 as the first office building in the city to achieve official "green" status from the U.S. Green Building Council (USGBC). The new structure is based within the six-story art deco Hearst building of the 1920s. Its architecture is defined by a triangular stainless-steel framing pattern, 80 percent of it recycled, that weighs about 20 percent less than a traditional steel frame. Rainwater collected on the roof and stored in a basement tank is used to replace water lost to evaporation in the building's air-conditioning system, to irrigate plants, and to fill the water sculpture in the main lobby. The ten-story atrium features escalators that run through a three-story water sculpture—a wide waterfall built with thousands of glass panels—that cools and humidifies the lobby air. The atrium floor is paved with heat-conductive limestone; polyethylene tubing embedded under the floor is filled with water that is circulated for cooling in the summer and heating in the winter. The building's façade is made up of low-E glass; light sensors on each floor determine the amount of artificial light necessary to balance the available natural light.

Opposite: The Condé Nast Building, at 4 Times Square in New York City, was one of the first commercial towers to utilize energy-saving features.

Photo: Courtesy of FXFOWLE Architects/Photographer: David Sundberg/Esto

The Bond is the nine-story headquarters building for the Lend Lease Corporation in downtown Sydney, Australia. The Bond features the use of chilled beams, which operate by pumping chilled water through cooling elements in the ceiling. The hot air from equipment and people below rises to the ceiling, is cooled by the chilled beams, and then falls, creating a natural convection process of hot air rising and cold air falling. The system significantly reduces energy consumption and greenhouse gas emissions.

Photos: (right and opposite, bottom) Courtesy of Lend Lease; (opposite, top) Gollings Photography/Courtesy of Lend Lease

The building has been designed to use 25 percent less energy than the minimum requirements for the city of New York and earned LEED Gold certification from the USGBC.

Designers around the globe are continually experimenting with technology to reduce energy consumption. For example, the façade of Barcelona's 35-story Agbar Tower is composed of two skins that, with glass blinds, reduce energy consumption in this warm climate and make optimal use of natural lighting.

The nine-story headquarters building for the Lend Lease Corporation in downtown Sydney, Australia, used an old technique, an eight-story atrium, to bring daylight to the building's interior. But the building's designers also specified a water-cooled air-conditioning system that is 30 percent more energy efficient than standard systems, using a natural ventilation system that draws in and filters outside air, then distributes it to each floor before venting it through the top of the building. Operable windows and

two external balconies on the western side of each floor expand ventilation options. Three sides of the building have external sunshades that respond to the movement of the sun (the fourth is shaded by neighboring buildings). Altogether, the building uses 30 to 40 percent less power than a standard Australian best-practices office building and emits 30 percent fewer greenhouse gases than a typical building.

Construction materials selected for the Lend Lease building had low and zero volatile organic compounds; they included natural materials such as bamboo and wood from sustainable forests. The sunshades were made from recycled timber from Walsh Bay wharves, and furnishings throughout the building have a high level of recycled content.

Building materials constitute a key aspect of sustainability. Buildings are composed of an extraordinary variety of materials that consume resources and energy and generate indoor and outdoor pollution in their manufacture, extraction, assembly into building components, transportation to and installation in or on the building, and even eventual replacement. Modular design, use of engineered wood products, reuse of salvaged materials, and recycling of waste from construction sites to improve sustainability are all becoming quite common. For example, during the development of Stapleton on the site of Denver's old airport, 1,100 acres (445 ha) of runway were recycled into more than 6 million tons of aggregate and used as a base for roads and sidewalks.

Advent of Rating Systems for Green Building

As interest and investment in green buildings have been growing across the United States, many designers have sought guidance to better understand what it takes to create green buildings—standards that could persuade their clients to adopt green features. Today, the USGBC is hailed as "the new best friend of corporate CEOs and Wall Street bankers" for having built a strong business case for green building practices.[7] In 1999, the USGBC unveiled a performance-measurement rating system for commercial, institutional, high-rise residential, and selected public building types that has transformed the design and construction of green buildings. One consultant group says the USGBC's LEED (Leadership in Energy and Environmental Design) rating system "took sustainable architecture out of the 'feel good' realm and made it understandable, quantifiable, and, most important, marketable."[8]

According to writer Charles Lockwood, who closely follows green building standards, the LEED system had led to certification of more than 800 projects and designers by early 2007. Developers vying for

Opposite: Elements at Kowloon Station, in Kowloon, Hong Kong, is a mixed-use retail, residential, and office development that is situated around transit and includes sustainable design elements. Seawater is used in the central air-conditioning system, and special glass is used to control solar energy gain from skylights and glass walls.

Photo: Grischa Ruschendorf

the status of certification had poured about 6,400 additional projects into the pipeline. By January 2007, 22 states and 74 local governments had adopted some level of LEED criteria for new and renovated public facilities.[9] The USGBC is expanding the coverage of its rating systems to make them applicable to almost all types of buildings.

Although LEED is being widely used, other rating systems are becoming known as well. Green Globes is administered by the Green Building Initiative, and the National Association of Home Builders has published "Model Green Homebuilding Guidelines." Also, individual city governments have adopted variations on LEED standards to guide their requirements for sustainable development.[10]

The LEED rating system lists criteria that allow a building to earn credits for incorporating specific features. Based on the total credits amassed, buildings may earn one of four levels of certification: bronze, silver, gold, or platinum. The USGBC makes awards after evaluating applications and documentation submitted by a building's designers and developers. The categories of criteria include planning for sustainable sites, improving energy efficiency, conserving materials and resources, enhancing environmental quality, safeguarding water, and improving the design and build process. Some of the categories have prerequisite criteria, and four offer bonus credits in addition to standard credits. The rating system permits choices among credits earned (except for the prerequisites).

Sustainability—More Than Green

Until recently, much of the emphasis in "thinking green" has focused on building design and construction. However, constructing greener buildings goes only partway toward achieving sustainable development. Greater attention to site planning and community design is critical to reducing the ecological footprint of urban development.

For example, the natural water cycle is typically disturbed by land development. Normally, rainfall filters into the ground, is transpirated from trees and vegetation into the air, or flows gradually into stream channels. Urban development that covers large areas with roofs and pavements sends most stormwater through drains into streams. Water runoff gushing into streams during and after storms aggravates streambank erosion and flooding conditions that can become quite destructive to the natural as well as the built environment.

Engineers and designers have mastered a number of techniques for supporting the natural water cycle even in densely developed areas of cities, where suburban-style detention ponds are impractical. In urban

Opposite: Green roofs, such as these on the Namba Parks retail center in Osaka, Japan, are aesthetically pleasing, insulate structures, and absorb rainwater.

Photo: The Jerde Partnership

areas, the guiding principle for sustainable stormwater management is to design for recharging it into the underground aquifer rather than detaining it on the surface. Recharging aquifers can be accomplished by direct infusion into the ground or by slowing the runoff rate to allow for infiltration and evaporation. Examples of such methods include promoting on-site rainwater infiltration by reducing pavement widths; providing porous (permeable) pavements; creating rain gardens, tree wells, and cisterns that infuse water into the ground; shaping landscape depressions and providing holding tanks under parking lots to temporarily store water; and absorbing runoff in grassed swales.

Green roofs provide another answer to the runoff problem and offer other contributions to green development as well. Increasingly used in European developments, green roofs are slowly gaining credibility in the United States for stormwater management, urban heat island reduction, building insulation, sound insulation, and the provision of green space. Green roofs are planted over thermal insulation and drainage layers, in a growing medium or modular planter boxes. Planted with grass, flowers, herbs, and even vegetables, green roofs absorb rainwater. The excess water can be transferred to holding basins on the site or under the building for infiltration into the water table. Plantings can be laid out to form gardens with sitting and recreation spaces as desired. Green roofs are being used for housing, office buildings, manufacturing plants, and civic buildings of all kinds. Some examples are Chicago's City Hall, Bonn's Art and Exhibition Hall in Germany, and Canberra's Parliamentary House in Australia. In China, a green rooftop project is blanketing rooftops with grasses to soak up rainwater, heat, and carbon dioxide, as well as reduce the buildings' energy consumption.

Understanding the importance of sustainable practices in development at the community scale, the USGBC, with the Congress for the New Urbanism and the National Resources Defense Council, has sponsored the formulation of a LEED rating process for developments at the neighborhood scale. Although some local jurisdictions have adopted similar types of performance standards for project evaluations or measures of program progress, the LEED-ND (Neighborhood Development) evaluation process provides a standardized system that can be applied in many communities. It measures the effects of projects on landscapes and neighborhood relationships, from site selection and land planning principles to the creative application of green construction and technology. Appropriately, in addition to rating green building practices, the LEED-ND process evaluates the extent to which proposed projects meet many of the guiding principles of smart growth described in chapter 2, including such factors as

■ Location adjacent to existing communities and infrastructure systems;
■ Protection of imperiled species, ecological communities, wetlands, and water bodies;
■ Compact development and diversity of uses;
■ Reduced automobile dependence and parking footprint; and
■ Access to public spaces and surrounding vicinity.

The LEED-ND process is being tested in a pilot program but is already viewed as an important tool for guiding community planning for future development.

Opposite: The 4,700-acre (1,900-ha) site of the former Stapleton Airport in Denver, Colorado, is being redeveloped as a sustainable, pedestrian-friendly, urban community.

Photo: Steve Larson

The range of sustainable development practices suggested by the LEED-ND criteria, as well as the guiding principles of smart growth, are exemplified in the Stapleton project on the site of Denver's old airport. Administered by the city in partnership with the Stapleton Redevelopment Foundation, Stapleton is striving to become a model of sustainable urban redevelopment. Planning for the 4,700-acre (1,900-ha) site enthusiastically embraced green building and the newest ideas for designing in-city neighborhoods. The adopted plan, described as a "Green Book" framework for redevelopment, declared the goal of developing "a network of urban villages, employment centers, and significant open space, all linked by a commitment to the protection of natural resources and the development of human resources."

A variety of housing types is being developed at Stapleton to encourage diversity of income, age, and household type.

Photo: Steve Larson

Forest City Enterprises was selected as master developer and by the fall of 2001, construction was underway on the first of 12,000 planned homes of all types, a green infrastructure system occupying one-third of the site, and schools and other public facilities. A proposed 10 million square feet (0.9 mil sq m) of office space, and shops, restaurants, and services in five town centers will generate on-site employment for an estimated 35,000 workers. In 2006 the first phase of Stapleton's 80-acre (32.4-ha) Central Park opened, and by 2008 its residents numbered 8,000.[11] Stapleton is a sustainable example of real urbanism. The community follows an urban pattern of pedestrian-friendly grid streets with residential districts located in walking distance of shopping, services, recreation, and employment. The mix of housing types provides residences for households of a wide range of incomes. Public

transportation connects the community to employment and other destinations beyond its edges. And it is knit into the surrounding community through compatible urban design and architecture.

The Clipper Mill development in Baltimore offers examples of several sustainability practices on a much smaller scale than Stapleton. Surrounded by an existing neighborhood, the development provides access to light rail with a stop at its entrance and shuttle services to other modes of public transit. The project renovated five historic industrial buildings and added new construction to create a mix of uses: 170 homes (townhouses, semidetached homes, condominiums, rental apartments), studio space for artists and craftspeople, and office and retail space. Sustainable features include a 1,600-square-foot (149-sq-m) green roof that forms the lawn of the courtyard for one of the residential buildings and a porous paving system for an office parking lot. Both techniques reduce and filter stormwater runoff and, in the case of the parking lot, discharge stormwater into the groundwater system rather than a nearby river. Clipper Mill's most innovative green feature is a living wall that filters air before returning it to the heating, ventilating, and air-conditioning system. Like Stapleton, Clipper Mill respects its neighborhood, its past, and the greater urban context through appropriate design and land use. (The project was one of ULI's 2007 Award for Excellence winners.)

The Uptown project is one of several that is helping to realize Oakland, California's goal to revitalize its downtown through urban-style

A mix of uses and distinctive park features help form a sense of place and create neighborhoods within Stapleton. Pictured: A fountain in one of the squares that highlight Stapleton's town center.

Photo: Steve Larson

redevelopment. Part of the city's goal is to draw 10,000 new residents into downtown, an area once dominated by surface parking lots and abandoned buildings. This compact, urban-style, mid-rise project is being developed by Forest City Enterprises, working with the city to remake Oakland in a more sustainable and livable mold.

The partnership is pursuing LEED Silver certification for its enclave of 665 rental apartments, 9,000 square feet (836 sq m) of retail space, and a public park, on a four-block site. One-quarter of the housing units are slated to be affordable housing. The project's sustainable strategies include the use of a remediated brownfield located one block from a rapid-transit station in a dense urban environment, with shopping and entertainment opportunities within easy walking distance. More than 90 percent of the construction waste from site demolition was reused or recycled, and at least 10 percent of the project's components will be made from recycled materials. At least 20 percent of construction materials will be manufactured within 500 miles (805 km) of the site. All adhesives, sealants, paints, and carpets will contain little to no volatile organic compounds. An integrated pest management system will be implemented to reduce or eliminate the use of pesticides in the buildings. Outside, water-efficient planting and irrigation will use about half as much water as conventional systems. Inside, energy-efficient lighting and appliances will conserve electricity, and low-flow showerheads and lavatory faucets will achieve a 20 percent reduction in water use.

Conclusion

Development in urban regions in the United States is intensifying pressures on vulnerable resources of land, water, air, wildlife, energy, and other elements of the physical environment while escalating social and economic inequities between developed and newly developing areas. Sustainability—green development—focuses on resource conservation in all spheres of the natural and built environments. Beyond protecting air and water quality, energy efficiency, and species habitats, sustainable development is concerned with providing adequate housing, medical care, and educational opportunities, and maintaining jobs and production of needed goods and services. Sustainable conservation of resources not only avoids the depletion of resources but also aims to improve them to accepted standards, to ensure their availability for future generations, while providing habitats at places and times that accommodate human needs and aspirations.

Designers have focused most on promoting sustainability by creating green buildings and more recently, through LEED-ND, have acknowledged the significance of considering broader site and neighborhood conditions. Real progress toward sustainable urbanism will require additional consideration of concentrated development that improves access to jobs, increases production of affordable housing, expands transportation options, and catalyzes other initiatives that promote the aims of smart growth. This is the holistic challenge of planning and design for sustainable communities.

1 Pew Center on Global Climate Change, *Towards a Climate-Friendly Built Environment* (Arlington, Va.: Pew Center, June 2005).

2 Presentation by Bruce Katz, Brookings Institution, "Blueprint for American Prosperity," November 6, 2007.

3 Jenifer Seal Cramer, "The Sustainable Frontier," *Urban Land Green*, Spring 2007, p. 23.

4 "Green Pieces," *Urban Land Green*, Spring 2007, p. 26.

5 "Our Common Future, Report of the World Commission on Environment and Development," World Commission on Environment and Development, 1987. Published as Annex to General Assembly document A/42/427, *Development and International Co-operation: Environment*, August 2, 1987.

6 *Remaking the Urban Waterfront* (Washington, D.C.: Urban Land Institute, 2004), p. 144.

7 Richard Fedrizzi, "Traffic Jam on the Frontier," *Urban Land Green*, Spring 2007 p. 99.

8 Dennis Jankiewicz, et al., "Agents of Change," *Urban Land Green*, Spring 2007, p. 96.

9 Charles Lockwood, "Green Building Standards Around the World," *Urban Land*, June 2007, p. 111.

10 For further information on LEED and other sustainable development rating systems, see Lockwood, "Green Building Standards Around the World," pp. 110–113; and Jim Miara, "LEED Versus Green Globes," *Urban Land*, June 2007, pp. 124–129.

11 Information from periodic reports about Stapleton's development by Forest City Enterprises and from www.stapletondenver.com.

Opposite: Sustainable features of the Clipper Mill project in Baltimore, Maryland, include easy access to a light-rail line, a green roof, and a living wall to purify air.

Photo: Patrick Ross Photography

PREPARING A PLAN and design concept for new development or for revitalization of existing development requires an understanding of the essential qualities of the site and its surroundings. Attorneys prepare cases by undertaking a discovery process, in which they identify the salient data and opinions that will direct their strategy for handling the case. For urban designers, discovery is a two-way street. The process gives the design team vital information

4 the discovery process

about the history and character of the neighborhood and its residents—all data that are important for recommending future development. At the same time, designers work with residents to identify opportunities that development may make available. Changes in the urban landscape are part of a continuum of adaptation to new circumstances, as ensuing generations of residents develop new needs and old ones fade away. The discovery process provides an opportunity for designers and planners to envision the evolution of an area, building on its strengths.

Discovery Begins at Home

Especially for urban infill and redevelopment sites, a designer's first obligation is to understand the past and present character of the area. Probing the past can illuminate perceptions of future opportunities. The origins of and creative trends in urban places suggest the direction of renewal. Rather than prescribe a packaged form of development for a site, designers need to explore the forces that brought people together there and shaped their environment. By framing the past, designers can envision it as the prologue to future development.

Mature street trees, contiguous buildings, and wide sidewalks with outdoor dining help make Barcelona's boulevards attractive.

Photos: Adrienne Schmitz

The Agbar Tower in Barcelona acts as a visual landmark along Avinguda Diagonal, a major thoroughfare leading to the Mediterranean Sea, and has become a symbol of Barcelona's revitalization.

Photo: Rafael Vargas

Barcelona, Spain, has evolved with an awareness that its urban character arises from multiple layers of elements that enrich the public domain and quality of life. Once an industrial city with a busy port, the city seized the opportunity of hosting the 1992 Olympics to launch a major campaign for civic improvement. Recognizing the value of history,

the effort built on the strength of Barcelona's original 1869 master plan by Ildefons Cerda, which remains the anchor for the city's unique block configuration and system of boulevards.

Even in Cerda's time, the city fathers made no attempt to remake the medieval sections of the city, so that today the interface of old and newly

Public art along the beach in Barcelona helps create a sense of place and orient pedestrians.

Photo: Zyscovich

built areas possesses a character unique to the city. In the 1980s, Barcelona's administrators set out to remake the city. Its urban planners respected Cerda's plan as a living document that was adaptable to serve modern life. They chose to invest their efforts in creating innovatively designed public spaces linked to infrastructure improvements of all kinds, generating redevelopment in previously dilapidated neighborhoods. Because the fundamental concepts of Cerda's plan are still being built out, it remains a contemporary guide to development. In the late 1990s, the city completed one of the original boulevards—El Diagonal—that terminates at the Mediterranean Sea and along which major new development has occurred. Urbanism based on a historic plan has been instrumental in Barcelona's ascension to the top rank of Europe's tourist destinations and centers for business investment.

Study Mapped Information

Time is never frozen in growing cities. Historic research and geographic data are powerful tools for demonstrating to stakeholders how urban design continuously evolves. Geographic information systems (GIS) software and documents such as maps, early aerial photographs, and plan drawings reveal how city planners anticipated future development.

Maps provide information about landownership, street patterns, and other geographic aspects of cities. A series of maps over time tell us how cities change. In the United States, the invaluable Sanborn maps of urban cores, originally assembled for insurance purposes and for many years updated periodically, depict building shapes and floor plans. They are especially useful for identifying changes that have already taken place in the built environment.

GIS mapping is widely available today and provides access to global data. GIS software programs can manipulate data to illustrate a wide variety of conditions and relationships in the urban scene. In a recent planning project, Zyscovich Architects used GIS mapping to identify property ownership, the age of structures, and building heights and through color coding gained an understanding of topographic conditions and concentrations of historic buildings. GIS mapping also revealed that real estate ownership in the area was in the hands of only a half-dozen families. The maps proved useful as a research tool and then as a description of findings for the stakeholders. Other sources of historic information are newspaper articles and historians and archivists—professional or amateur. Anecdotal information from local history buffs can be a rich resource for data that are not recorded.

Get the Story Straight

Families, homes, and commercial buildings can be counted, and the U.S. Bureau of the Census can provide plenty of other hard data. But it is just as important to ask, what are the real stories of the people and the place? For example, what interests are at stake—property ownership, familiarity with the area, long-term relationships with neighborhood people and organizations? Are residents or businesses likely to be displaced by new development? If so, what economic and psychological impacts might they experience—loss of jobs or relationships, difficulties in relocating, moving expenses? The outlook of current residents may well generate resistance to new development unless design approaches are sensitive to their concerns.

Alternatively, in what ways can existing residents add value to the redeveloped area as prospective tenants or owners for new homes, or as owners of businesses that would strengthen the community? What physical assets and amenities would provide an enticing environment for new development? For example, are there forgotten and overgrown parks that could be rescued, or stands of trees that could be preserved, or attractive views that could become selling points for redeveloped areas? Framing the story of the past helps

The Cap is a retail project in Columbus, Ohio, that sits atop a highway overpass and connects the downtown and the city's arts district. The architecture of the buildings ties the project into the surrounding area.

Photo: Meleca Architecture

current residents recognize their role in the larger life of a place, gives them a sense of ownership in the planning process, and makes change less intimidating.

Make Connections Across Boundaries

As in baseball, "home" is only one of the bases in the field of play for invigorating urban neighborhoods. Designers concerned with creating real urbanism reach out to discover the resources beyond the immediate area. Commercial centers and civic services in the vicinity might serve needs in the revitalized area. Stable neighborhoods nearby may act as anchors for new development, and their design attributes may suggest desirable features for revitalization. In their master plan for the City West HOPE VI redevelopment in Cincinnati, Ohio, the design team

of Torti-Gallas and Partners and Stalls and Lee Architects drew on the features of a successfully restored historic neighborhood just a few blocks away. Not only did local residents admire the handsome designs for redevelopment, but the developer of the new homes also found that the presence of the historic homes strengthened the market for the mixed-income project. Establishing clear sightlines to well-known civic buildings, churches, and other landmark structures can establish place-making qualities to help spur revitalization.

Connections with adjacent areas can be turned inward as well. Extensions of street patterns to or from adjacent areas can emphasize real as well as virtual connections with existing neighborhoods. The inward-focused superblocks of public housing in the City West area, which effectively isolated it from surrounding neighborhoods, were

redesigned to highlight a street system that connected the neighbor-hoods. The grid street system in place around the Midtown Miami devel-opment described in chapter 1 provided a model for on-site street design that reconnected old to new.

Consider the Market

Revitalization requires a sober identification of the qualities of urbanism that can be successful in the location and with the resources at hand. This requires asking a multitude of questions: Who will choose to live in the area? What are the market forces in play? Are previously unrecog-nized opportunities opening up? What advantages does the location

Understanding the market was key to the success of Market Creek Plaza in San Diego, California. The center replaced an abandoned factory with a commercial and cultural center in an ethnically diverse city neighborhood.

Photo: The Jacobs Center for Neighborhood Innovation

confer on future residents and businesses? What types of residential buildings and retail spaces can they afford? What services and amenities will they demand?

After an arduous process of assembling funding and organizational support, Cleveland's rejuvenated Lee-Harvard neighborhood shopping center reasserted its role as a valued feature of the middle-class neighborhoods around it. Following years of decline in the once-flourishing center's physical conditions and in the goods and services it offered, neighborhood organizations brought together a collaborative public/private development team that reconfigured the center and attracted new businesses. The effort bet on the continued strength of the inner-city market

A community-based design process resulted in the development of Highlands' Garden Village in Denver, Colorado.

Photo: Aero Arts

and benefited from the team's strategic decisions about the desirable mix of services and the visual identity of the center. Now an attractive shopping venue once again, it enables area residents to shop locally for their daily needs instead of traveling miles to other parts of the region.

Highlands' Garden Village is a mixed-use, mixed-income infill development in Denver, Colorado, planned as a socioeconomically diverse community—in the developers' words, "to demonstrate the economic benefits of mixing incomes, product types, and uses." Developed by Chuck Perry and Jonathan F. P. Rose on the 27-acre (11-ha) site of a former amusement park, the village arose from a community-based design process that aimed to blend new development with the older neighborhoods surrounding the site. Completed in 2007 after eight years of work, the neighborhood comprises 306 residential units, 130,000 square feet (12,000 sq m) of commercial and civic uses, and 3.2 acres (1.3 ha) of parks and gardens. The residential units vary in type, design, and price, to serve a broad market. For example, 40 percent of the apartments were designated as affordable units and 20 of the single-family homes include an apartment atop the garage as an affordable rental option. To help reach this extended market, the city granted special zoning, a density bonus, tax increment financing of infrastructure, and housing assistance funds. The project was selected by ULI as a 2007 award winner.[1]

Engage the Stakeholders

By proposing changes in the status quo, development—and especially redevelopment—raises issues and stirs uncertainty among current residents. For that reason, major decisions on development projects are seldom made these days without consulting the people most directly involved, including area residents, business owners, and civic leaders, as well as the local governmental officials and staff who administer the policies and regulations that affect development. There are good reasons for paying attention to their views, which often reflect worries about their evolving communities—more traffic, school overcrowding, resident displacement, rising housing costs, poorly kept parks and playgrounds, loss of valued open space, all seemingly beyond control. Also, development projects are becoming more complicated, as are the regulations guiding them. Public decisions about development require difficult choices, and many citizens distrust both the developers and those who administer development regulations.

Engaging the people who are most directly affected by proposed development can result in the creation of a shared vision. The key for designers is to turn distrust into hope by proposing and committing to a clear vision for the project. Change becomes more acceptable when it is shown to be occurring within an evolving context of urban development, as a natural occurrence in the growth of cities and in response to the changing needs of successive generations. Many people find it difficult to imagine beneficial changes resulting from development, and they are often outspoken about their concerns and objections. The designer's job is to listen carefully, acknowledge fears or misunderstandings, and demonstrate a willingness to address their concerns and consider alternatives and new ideas.

To create a socioeconomically diverse community, Highlands' Garden Village contains a mix of housing types: single-family, townhouses, live/work, cohousing, and rental apartments for senior citizens.

Photo: Rose Companies

Honesty remains the best policy: the potential downsides of a proposal should be acknowledged and weighed against the positive aspects, not hidden behind a verbal blizzard. Openness about the consequences of a plan or design is necessary to secure trust. Working with the depth of information derived from studying the past and present conditions of the site and surrounding neighborhood, the point person for the discussion should be able to describe positive aspects of the proposal that can mitigate unwanted effects. Above all, the professional advisers involved in the discussions should shun technical parlance and tendencies to overwhelm or talk down to participants.

In my experience, the preferred mode of discussion is a forum, or community "conversation" for soliciting ideas and generating interchange among participants. Many architects and urban planners stage charrettes, which focus on brainstorming sessions in which participants from the community can control the direction of the design. Without expert

The plan for redeveloping a hurricane-stricken neighborhood of **New Orleans, Louisiana,** involved extensive public input and focused on the historical context of each area.

Graphic: Zyscovich

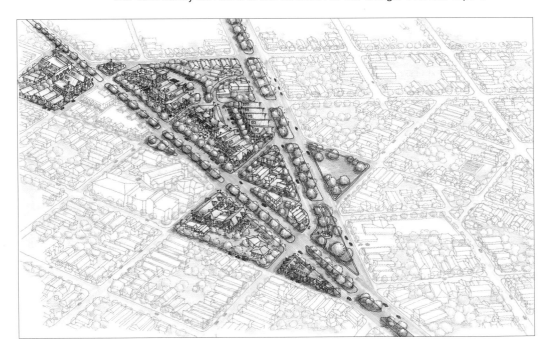

guidance, though, such sessions can disregard hard data and overlook the realities of market potential and financing. Too many of these gatherings establish unrealistic expectations, formulating wish lists that in the end cannot be fulfilled. Because the leadership role is reserved for the development team, community conversations allow for better interaction without requiring immediate commitments to specific design solutions. They offer ways to broach and test ideas in an informal situation. Such a forum adds the dimension of expertise by providing comments from a

panel of experts and a moderated discussion that balances participants' desires and expectations with professional assessments of practicality. The combination of educated dialogue and free-flowing, relatively informal conversations leads to realistic plans and designs that obtain the buy-in of community residents and leaders.

Community participation was an integral element in the development of the FEC strategic redevelopment plan described in chapter 1. Community conversations were held in each neighborhood within the redevelopment area. They proved critical to interpreting the results of basic research, especially in the articulation of potential assets that could contribute to neighborhood growth and vitality. Two rounds of neighborhood workshops engaged residents and other stakeholders in the planning process and helped designers develop a fuller understanding of the issues, needs, and aspirations of each neighborhood. At the second set of meetings, participants drew "concept maps" that eventually were folded into the draft FEC plan.

Involvement in community conversations does not always follow an easy course. Some of the most complex and difficult conversations took place in New Orleans after Hurricane Katrina. Zyscovich Architects was brought in to create urban restoration plans for five of the 49 flooded neighborhoods. In some, residents had organized and completed analyses of their neighborhoods; in others, not a single person had been contacted by officials from any agency. The community conversations we

The inclusion of parks and greenways was considered vital for improving the quality of life in New Orleans after Hurricane Katrina.

Graphic: Zyscovich

organized then became the first opportunity for residents to express their needs. The first contacts demonstrated that residents' minds were understandably focused on the considerable problems of daily life and subsistence rather than long-term community planning. Before any meaningful conversation about the long-term prospects for neighborhood improvement or redevelopment, residents needed an effective

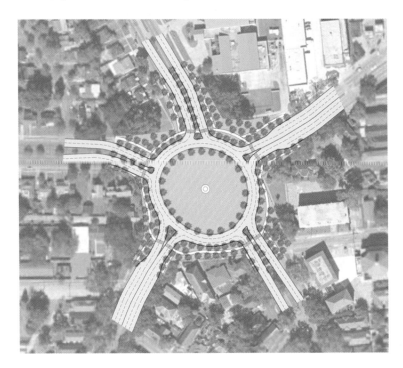

means of speaking out about their more immediate concerns. Numerous community workshops were held in order to hear residents spell out the precise nature and scope of those concerns.

One of the most difficult aspects of this effort was determining who represented whom and the breadth of their representation. Another difficulty was locating neutral meeting places that did not raise issues of territorial distrust, because the neighborhoods were quite distinct in character. Many meetings required the services of a local facilitator, a civic leader, and representatives of respected organizations to help guide the discussions. Public announcements aired on cable television and a locally focused Web site spread awareness of the meetings and presentations.

From this beginning, neighborhood planning networks—essentially citizen subcommittees—were formed to determine priorities concerning residential, health care, and security issues. As a result, the plans underscored the urgency of stabilizing basic conditions of neighborhood infrastructure (such as clearing debris, repairing streets and street lighting) and restoring public services provided by schools, health care centers, police stations, and libraries. Each neighborhood's history and cultural origins suggested directions for improvements. For example, the 7th Ward was originally inhabited by the craftsmen—bricklayers, ironworkers, roofers, decorative artists—who built the houses of the French Quarter. Descendants of these craftsmen continue to live there. The plan for reviving the 7th Ward emphasized restoring it as a vocational and craft center. Based on residents' suggestions, a goal was added to encourage the return of the local music culture, including street musicians, young musicians, and the music of street funerals.

Plans for each of the neighborhoods were drawn up in collaboration with residents. The $750 million provided by the U.S. Department of Housing and Urban Development, the Federal Emergency Management Administration (FEMA), and state agencies has been allocated according to each neighborhood's specific needs, and plans are in various stages of implementation. The city of New Orleans has also issued requests for bids on contracts for miscellaneous FEMA-eligible sidewalk and roadway repairs at various locations, typically along the smaller streets within neighborhoods. The strategy is to promote building in the first 17 targeted recovery zones around public assets in business corridors, in an effort to generate further private investment from developers. Three types of recovery zones are involved:

- "Rebuild areas," which have experienced severe destruction of physical structures and social networks, requiring major rebuilding and significant public and private investment in order to recover;

- "Redevelop areas," which have some recovery components and resources and have a high potential for attracting private investment and acting as a catalyst for further redevelopment; and

- "Renew areas," in which specific projects that require relatively modest public intervention can be initiated to supplement work that is already underway by the private and nonprofit sectors.

Do the Math

Solidly grounded data is the primary requirement for engaging stakeholders. The initial facts and figures about neighborhood trends emerge from earnest study of the past and present conditions in the area. But discussions with stakeholders will yield more information, often at a finer grain than the dry statistics. This information from the people most affected will help shape designs that truly respond to local needs. No project should generate consequences that diminish the quality of

Opposite: Reinvigorating and greening traffic circles is a key aspect of neighborhood reconstruction in New Orleans.

Graphic: Zyscovich

life in the area; instead, all should accommodate community interests and, at best, enhance the public realm.

Most important, good data will help people see proposals as fundamentally believable and attainable. Getting the numbers right—about the scale of development and redevelopment, about its effects on the neighborhood's quality of life (such as traffic generation, distance to schools, and access to parks and services), and about public costs and private gains—will provide concrete reasons for supporting proposals. Much discussion in the East Cambridge planning process described in chapter 2 centered on the traffic congestion that would stem from substantial new development. The consultants ran the numbers and suggested sources of relief (shopping within walking distance, additional transit service), but their data showed without a doubt that further development would generate more traffic. However, they observed that additional traffic might be a small price to pay for substantial improvements in the neighborhood's quality of life, in the form of better housing, more parks, prettier streetscapes, and greater proximity to jobs. Based on the numbers and the improvements that the plan demonstrated, community representatives bought into that argument.

The community of Atlantic Beach, South Carolina, had to understand the math involved in working out redevelopment plans that promised to improve the local economy. The community was one of few recreational havens for African Americans during nearly a century of racial segregation. Founded in the 19th century by slaves known as the Gullah or Geechee (with their own language, which is still spoken by older residents), Atlantic Beach from the 1930s onward was a hub for black businesses, vacationers, and entertainers. Today it is one of only two black-owned and black-governed oceanfront towns on the east coast.

Unlike neighboring communities, Atlantic Beach had kept visual and physical access to the oceanfront by retaining property ownership within families over time and resisting proposals for rezoning to allow development. But regulatory restraints that had successfully preserved the beachfront's natural beauty had also throttled opportunities for feasible development by preventing the consolidation of the typically small lots into developable sites. By 2005, the town was in serious need of tax revenue to support even minimal public services. When several properties were sold to developers who announced intentions to build high-rise apartments, the stage was set for contentious reconsideration of zoning restrictions. Although many townspeople wanted to spur beachfront redevelopment to improve the community's economic standing, many also wished to retain the town's historic identity and physical character.

Opposte: The municipality of Atlantic Beach, South Carolina, posed redevelopment challenges that were best addressed with various levels of allowable beachfront development. The redevelopment plan for Atlantic Beach focused on balancing economic growth with the preservation of the town's historic character.

Graphic: Zyscovich

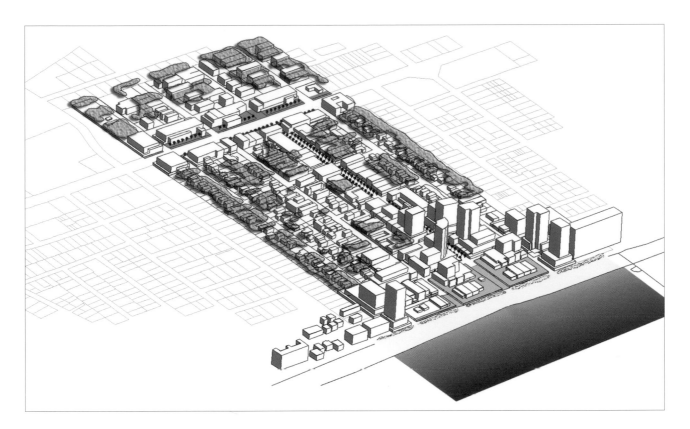

Zyscovich Architects was brought in to assist in thinking through a development strategy and rezoning process.

Establishing the firm's credentials was our first order of business. We were open and frank about what we knew and didn't know—and how we would proceed to find out. We enlisted an African-American economist whom we had worked with on several projects, who was able to portray market projections in concrete terms. After the first meeting our staff sat with the community, relaxing in chairs rather than lecturing from a podium, which made the discussion more conversational. Working with a steering committee, the firm described the types of development allowed by existing zoning and suggested several alternatives to the provisions that would allow various scales of new construction. Over almost a year, after many discussions with the steering committee and three townwide "conversations," the steering committee reached agreement on the scale of development to be pursued. The town council approved a master plan that included recommendations for zoning changes.

Always Touch Base with Officialdom

Seeking participation by local residents, businesses, and community leaders in the planning and design process can establish local support for development, but the process cannot ignore the public officials who are responsible for maintaining community stability and livability. Leaving them out of the information flow is almost always a deal killer. Elected officials and administrators can be called upon to join in community conversations or even lead some discussions, if they can do so in a collaborative manner without political posturing. Smart officials and departmental staff will want to stay informed about the tenor and direction of the discussions and therefore will be eager to hear constituents' concerns and ideas. They can prove useful in reminding participants of the purposes of previously adopted policies and plans and the need for even-handed decision making.

The discovery process must include fostering an understanding of citywide concerns and potential citywide benefits from development and redevelopment in particular neighborhoods. Those involved in community conversations should be made aware of the broader civic interests at stake and, for that matter, the tangible civic support (in the form of ongoing programs and budget allocations) that may affect decisions on proposed development.

Expect Re-Visioning

The final plan or design seldom falls neatly into place. As designers study the area and talk to local officials, they may grasp some big ideas about the scale and content of future development that can form major goals or a prospective vision for the project. Based on these ideas, the professional staff may begin to rough out some prototype features of potential development. But they also know that they will learn more as the community conversations reveal more information and begin to establish stakeholders' major concerns. In the process, some of the big ideas may fall by the wayside while others may achieve greater prominence. And as the details of the pros and cons of various features become more evident, the details of the proposal will evolve as well. The vision will be revisited and refashioned as participants begin to focus on their real priorities for the development. The issue in the Atlantic Beach rezoning discussions, for example, turned on the potential effects of various levels of beachfront development on the townspeoples' visual and physical enjoyment of the beach.

In this milieu, an important role for discussion leaders is to keep the key goals of the project front and center, constantly relating participants' suggestions and proposals to the major objectives. At the same time, the design team must work toward resolving issues as they arise, if necessary through small, focus-group discussions that permit participants

Opposite: Atlantic Beach's redevelopment plan called for more parks, improved streetscapes, and infill development to boost the local economy.

Graphic: Zyscovich

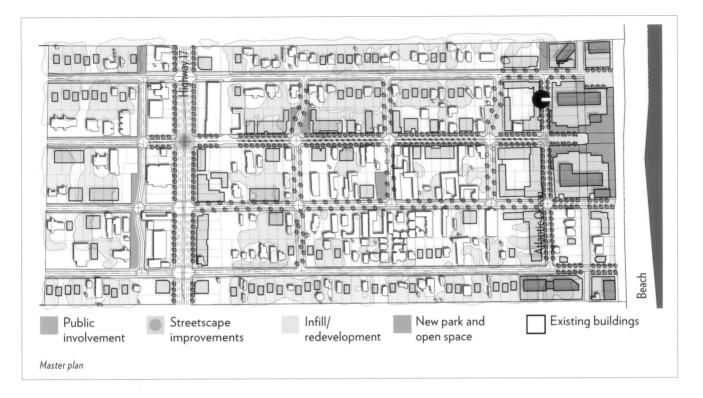

| ■ Public involvement | ● Streetscape improvements | Infill/ redevelopment | New park and open space | □ Existing buildings |

Master plan

to concentrate on learning and making decisions about technical aspects of the project. For example, the East Cambridge design process included a number of highly technical discussions with a small group about traffic and transit issues. Thus agreement on a plan or design stems from the process of participants acquiring and applying knowledge to agree on decisions, eventually reaching consensus on a vision and the specific character of the development.

Conclusion

Discovery results from exploration. Important information is gained relating to the character of areas to be developed or redeveloped, the concerns of the local populace and the public officials responsible for promoting improvements, market demands, and the possible futures that may be envisioned. In creating or recreating desirable, real urbanism, designers and planners undertake a voyage of discovery with all the fervor and excitement promised by every voyage into unknown territory. It is a collaborative expedition to a goal that is increasingly clarified by the knowledge they acquire en route.

1 "Highlands' Garden Village," in *Award Winning Projects 2007* (Washington, D.C.: Urban Land Institute, 2007), pp. 92–94.

CREATING A SHARED VISION and expressing it in a development plan or design is hard, time-consuming work that requires the kind of collaboration, creativity, and trust described in the previous chapter. But creating the vision is merely the starting point. Nurturing and translating a vision into action, especially for large, complex projects, requires numerous steps and, typically, many years of implementation. Furthermore, in most cities, the project vision, plan, and implementation

5   public framework and vision

process occurs within a larger context of citywide comprehensive planning policies, neighborhood and commercial corridor plans, zoning and subdivision regulations, building codes, and other ordinances and requirements. As cities have increasingly addressed concerns about environmental sustainability, smart growth, and other concepts of "good growth," they have added to the complexity of the public framework for development.

All the more reason, therefore, for cities to establish forward-looking land use and urban design plans and policies for key development and redevelopment areas and sites. Such a planning process can focus intently on designing solutions for specific area characteristics and needs. To create this more detailed public framework for development, both public and private clients frequently employ urban planners and designers to prepare area plans and recommend public policies, regulations, and action programs.

The East Cambridge plan and design provided the necessary policy context for developers to proceed with major redevelopment projects and for the city to program neighborhood public improvements. For the Midtown Miami and FEC projects, Zyscovich Architects drew up an overall plan that highlighted redevelopment opportunities in the Bayfront area and

then focused on delineating a specific plan for a key redevelopment site and proposing zoning regulations and urban design guidelines to guide the development process. We also recommended specific infrastructure improvements, including a new street system and restoration of a historic streetcar line that would support future development.

This chapter focuses on the ways in which urban designers can participate in the establishment of a public framework (ideally reflecting a community vision) that will assist in translating design goals into desirable developments. Essentially, the framework expresses the public

New construction in Miami Beach has been scaled and designed to complement the historic Art Deco District architecture while adding 21st-century excitement.

Photo: Zyscovich

interests in pursuing a development. It can also guide the public, private, and public/private investments needed to support development. Six examples from designers acting within and contributing to the public framework are described in the following pages.

Planning for Hollywood's Young Circle Redesign

The city of Hollywood, located on the Atlantic Ocean between Fort Lauderdale and Miami, was founded by Joseph Young, who arrived from California in 1920 to turn tomato fields and marshland into his "dream city." Although the city's early growth was slowed by a major hurricane, the stock market crash of 1929, and World War II,

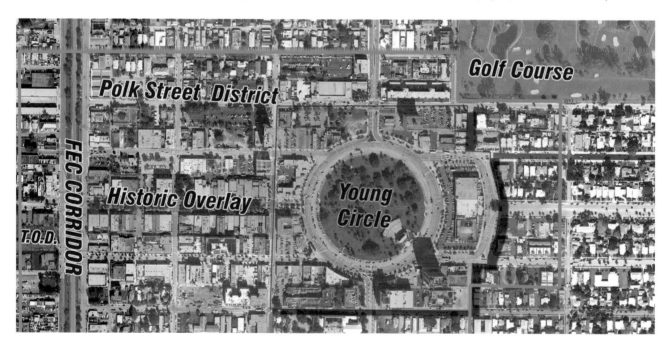

Young Circle was the primary focus of the urban regeneration plan for Hollywood, Florida. Zoning recommendations and design standards were part of a broader design study. Today the iconic circle has been revitalized as an exciting, pedestrian-friendly public space.

Graphic: Zyscovich

Hollywood's development surged rapidly in the 1950s and today the city is a mature community of more than 130,000 residents. The city's layout features Hollywood Boulevard, a major thoroughfare stretching from the oceanfront inland to the Everglades. This central avenue intersects with and encircles three large parks. The easternmost, Young Circle and the ten-acre (4.3-ha) park within it, is an iconic element of downtown Hollywood. Until recently, however, low-density commercial outlets, parked cars, and the wide boulevard blocked views of this "arts park" and created obstacles for pedestrians trying to access it.

The city adopted a new master plan, crafted in 2005 and 2006, calling for revitalization of the city's center. The park was upgraded to

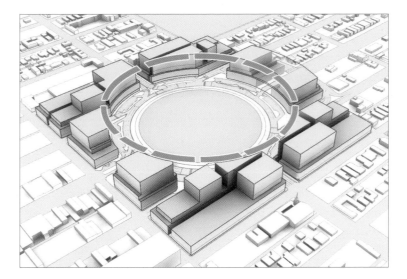

feature a central fountain and extensive plantings, including baobab and palm trees, that form a setting for art exhibits. Subsequently, the city commissioned the Zyscovich firm to prepare a plan, zoning recommendations, and design standards for the Young Circle area as part of a broader design study. After extensive discussions and several public forums involving community and business leaders as well as residents, we developed a plan to guide private sector proposals for commercial redevelopment and for the expansion of the arts and cultural facilities clustered in and around Young Circle.

The plan was based on an overall vision to heighten the synergy of Young Circle by enhancing its pedestrianism, within and around the park as well as in existing and new retail and restaurant venues along the outer edge of the circle. The plan's key proposals are as follows:

- Capitalize on existing and planned arts and cultural resources by augmenting existing buildings with new structures and activities and improving the physical interconnections between them and the community around Young Circle.
- Create a safer environment for pedestrians by moving parking from the periphery of the park to the outer edge of the circle, where it would front directly on planned commercial development, and separating it from traffic lanes with a shaded pedestrian promenade that would shorten pedestrians' crossing distance to the park.
- Reinforce the circular form by developing buildings that front the circle with curved façades to trace its edge.
- Open up visual connections between Young Circle and the Hollywood Golf Course to the north, by means of a public network of green corridors and parks.

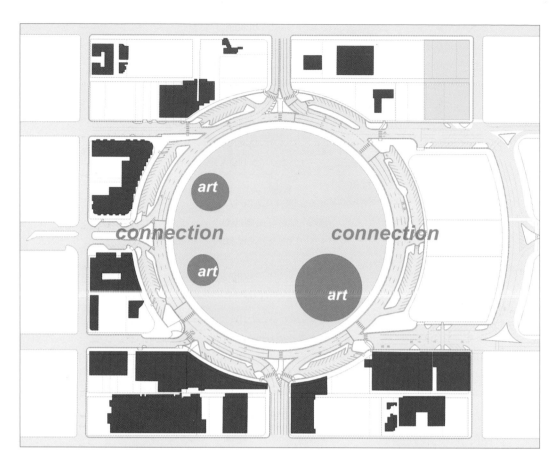

connection   *connection*

art

art

art

A goal of the Young Circle park renovation was to create a space for public art exhibits with easy connections to the surrounding city.

Graphic: Zyscovich

- Extend the streetscape of Hollywood Boulevard farther west to enhance connections to the historic downtown and stimulate greater commercial activity along the boulevard.

The Zyscovich firm recommended design standards that would improve the quality of architectural design and public spaces in and around Young Circle and the downtown area. These standards are being used in the city's zoning approval process for new development. The recommendations stated that development should meet the needs of pedestrians, such as using awnings, colonnades, arcades, and canopy trees to create more shade; widening sidewalks with decorative paving and entry plazas and making room for café seating for restaurants; and placing richly detailed building façades on the ground floors to establish a lively and interesting pedestrian environment. To ensure high-quality and varied building designs that augment the street's character, we recommended alignment with the "build-to" line, to follow the natural curve of the circle, as well as heights of no more than 15 stories, protection of view corridors along Federal Highway and Hollywood Boulevard, varied and memorable building façades, articulated building masses, frontage uses for parking garages, and special attention to signage and lighting.

New zoning regulations also recommended that current zoning districts be replaced with a Young Circle Special District. The major change is an application of requirements for each city block rather than for building frontages; the geometry of the properties and blocks is irregular and many buildings have and will have multiple building frontages. In addition, appropriate uses vary from block to block. Highlights of the proposed zoning include the following:

- The purposes and permitted uses remain largely in place.
- Floor/area ratio standards encourage higher densities and building heights along the Young Circle frontage and lower heights along other frontages.
- More specific setbacks are required by build-to lines that promote the design standards recommended for the circle.
- Building height bonuses can be awarded if the developer includes public uses or benefits such as historic preservation and spaces for public use.
- As-of-right height limits were raised to 15 stories and a maximum floor/area ratio of 3.75 was established, although to reach the maximum limits the city council is considering requirements for affordable units and other special needs.

Parking was moved from the periphery of the park to the outer edge of Young Circle to be closer to commercial establishments and to facilitate pedestrian access.

Graphic: Zyscovich

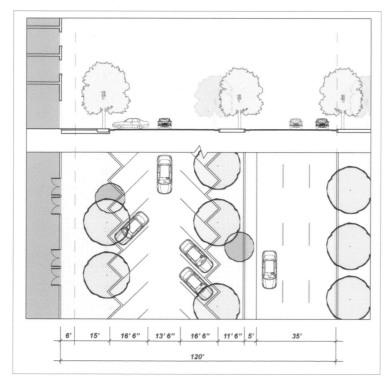

| 6' | 15' | 16' 6" | 13' 6" | 16' 6" | 11' 6" | 5' | 35' |

120'

Young Circle's renovation and landscaping have revitalized a key park in Hollywood. In addition, a framework has been established to guide the nature of development around the circle.

Photo: Zyscovich

- Parking structures fronting the circle must incorporate usable front-age space ("liner units"), and this requirement is "encouraged" for parking structures on other major streets in the area.
- Rehabilitations of historic structures are granted additional building height and transfer of allowable floor/area ratios within the block in which the historic structures are located.
- Parking requirements do not apply to uses in the first and second floors of buildings, and shared parking is allowed.
- Special design standards are imposed in the Hollywood Boulevard and Taylor Street overlay districts to protect the existing quality of development.

The city adopted the proposed plan and design standards for Young Circle in 2006. Improvements by mid-2008 included the renovation and landscaping of the Arts Park and shifting of on-street parking to the outer edge of the circle along the commercial frontage. Two redevelopment projects fronting the circle were underway, and other owners of properties fronting the circle were preparing plans for redevelopment. The new development regulations reinforce the form and mass of the park while elevating the character and quality of development around it. Most important, the improvements highlight the function of Young Circle as an important gateway to Hollywood's downtown area.

Revitalizing a University-Based Neighborhood in Columbus, Ohio

The Ohio State University created Campus Partners for Community Urban Redevelopment in 1995 to spearhead the revitalization of urban neighborhoods and the High Street commercial corridor around the campus. Not only is High Street the "main street" of Columbus, it also runs for nearly two miles (3.2 km) through the heart of the university district adjoining the campus. However, the corridor had suffered from three decades of disinvestment: surface parking lots had replaced buildings, bars had displaced other services, and students and other residents had turned elsewhere for housing, shopping, and entertainment. Surrounding neighborhoods had also declined.

One of the prime strategies for improving conditions in the university district was to enhance the economic vitality of High Street. In 1995 and 1996 Campus Partners directed a community-based planning

The South Campus Gateway project on High Street near Ohio State in Columbus, Ohio, is a showcase for using public, institutional, and private actors to revitalize a commercial strip and a neighborhood.

Photo: Brad Feinknopf

Outdoor seating and
public plazas have helped
reinvigorate a key corridor in
Columbus.

Photo: Brad Feinknopf

process that resulted in the adoption of a revitalization concept plan in 1997. Campus Partners then formed a 40-person advisory committee and employed Goody Clancy, a Boston-based architecture firm, to conduct a detailed study and prepare a revitalization plan.

"A Plan for High Street: Creating a 21st-Century Main Street" proposed public and private actions to enhance the civic and commercial vitality of High Street, create new economic opportunities, and reinforce High Street as an environment that supports learning. To accomplish these goals, the plan recommended the adoption of development and design guidelines and a commercial zoning overlay, the establishment of a parking management entity to manage parking as a system, and the formation of a special improvement district to support improvements in the public realm and manage strategic redevelopment efforts. With support from Campus Partners, the plan is being implemented successfully. A few results:

- The Columbus city council adopted an urban commercial zoning overlay for High Street in 2001 and the plan for High Street and development design guidelines in 2002.
- A homeownership incentive program has been created to encourage Ohio State faculty and staff to buy and live in homes in the university district. The program had attracted 90 employees to the nearby neighborhoods by 2007.
- Ohio State constructed the Schoenbaum Family Center as an early-childhood laboratory in a neighborhood setting. The university established a partnership with the public schools that serve the district to promote them as models of urban education. University students, faculty members, and staff members are involved in learning, health care, and education in family living skills and job readiness.
- Substantial improvements to municipal services such as refuse collection, street sweeping, and code enforcement have taken place.
- The city initiated a storefront-façade improvement program that provides grants and loans for improvements along High Street.

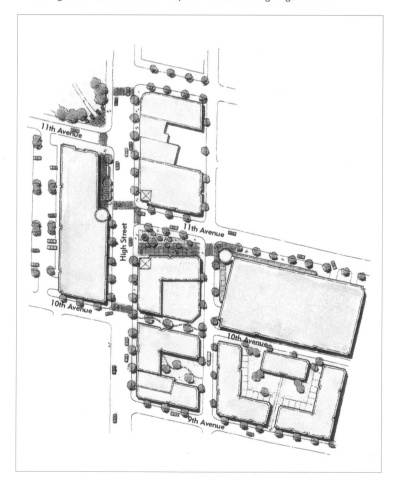

South Campus Gateway site plan.

Graphic: Goody Clancy

- Campus Partners redeveloped a 7.5-acre (3-ha) parcel on High Street as a mixed-use development; opened in 2005, it includes several retail stores and restaurants, office space, 184 apartments, and a 1,200-space parking garage.
- The city and the university funded a study starting in 2004 to prepare a streetscape improvement plan for High Street.
- The Ohio Capital Corporation for Housing was brought in by Campus Partners to acquire 1,335 units of Section 8 housing in need of extensive renovation within the university district. That work began in 2004.
- Campus Partners worked with the city and community groups to prepare a plan for the Weinland Park neighborhood. Adopted in 2006, the plan included the redevelopment of a 21-acre (8.5-ha) brownfield site for market-rate housing and a community park.[1]

The 7.5-acre (3-ha) South Campus Gateway project is the centerpiece of a broader High Street revitalization project.

Photo: Brad Feinknopf

Transforming Miami's South Beach

Securing great design takes many forms, not least the activism of engaged citizens. The great transformation in South Beach since the late 1970s was driven by a citizenry that recognized the value of its architectural heritage and was determined to protect it. Ironically, the neighborhood now known as the Art Deco District in Miami Beach had suffered years of economic decline. Developers paid no attention to the area, and the city's strategy to revive the neighborhood was oriented to demolition and rebuilding rather than to renovation and preservation. Barbara Capitman, a visionary, championed the architectural value of the neighborhood, pulling together artists, designers, and other visionaries to help make the case for preservation. With her relentless drive for publicity, Capitman attracted the attention of national architectural publications, founded the Miami Design Preservation League, organized the annual Art Deco Weekend and, with her family, invested in the creation of a café in the Carlyle Hotel, an art deco masterpiece on Ocean Drive. The café quickly became a gathering place for preservation activities. Capitman also solicited the Princeton architectural firm of Robert Venutri and Denise Scott Brown to conduct a study of the major commercial artery, Washington Avenue. That was followed by a master

Along Miami Beach's Ocean Drive, historic art deco buildings continue to be restored.

Photo: Thorn Grafton

planning project by Anderson, Knotter, Feingold. These efforts helped generate the nomination of the one-square-mile district for the National Register of Historic Places in 1979.

In the 1980s, artists and young people began moving into the neighborhood, drawn by the cheap beachfront apartments. Their cosmetic changes, such as painting the buildings in pastel colors, attracted the fashion and television industries. Soon, local politicians began to recognize the area's potential and supported the funding that established the Miami Beach Community Development Corporation in 1981. As a result, a historic district was established along the picturesque and historic Espanola Way and public funding for façade and streetscape improvements for neighborhood businesses was obtained. South Beach's revitalization evolved one building at a time.

Still, the City Commission remained reluctant to impede redevelopment, and oceanfront properties between 15th and 23rd streets and along historic Lincoln Road continued to be available for rebuilding. The small, incremental successes upon which Barbara Capitman depended, coupled with wide media attention, ultimately swelled public concern and spurred the adoption of a local preservation ordinance in the early 1980s. New regulations came into effect as the result of negotiations between the city and the Miami Design Preservation League to support construction of a much-needed convention and resort hotel in return for the establishment of a historic preservation district along Ocean Drive, to be known as the Miami Beach Art Deco

Opposite: Public and private actors have cooperated to revitalize Miami Beach, Florida. One key project was the restoration of the historic St. Moritz Hotel (at right) as part of the Loews Hotel project.

Below: View of Anchor Shops at the intersection of Washington and 16th streets, looking toward the Loews Hotel.

Photos: Steven Brooke

District. Under the League's direction, sidewalks were widened, streetscapes improved, and the entry-level floors of older hotels were converted to cafés and restaurants. People thronged to the neighborhood and developer interest surged. In time the city's economy responded to the area's regained international prominence as a tourist destination and residential enclave.

South Beach has steadily continued to evolve. In 2001, the city of Miami Beach initiated an update of the Convention Center District through a Community Redevelopment Agency. The work included preparation of a ten-year master plan for a six-acre (2.4-ha) site in the Convention Center District, which is part of the historic district established in 1992. It has become the cultural, recreational, and commercial core of South Beach. Of particular interest was the siting of a state-of-the-art facility to house the Miami Beach New World Symphony and its teaching, performance, broadcasting, and rehearsal spaces. The preliminary concept plan, developed by Zyscovich Architects, anticipates the creation of a 21st-century town center, an emblematic civic space for South Beach. The plan updates a 1993 plan for the city's center and integrates several proposals made in previous city-sponsored planning studies, including streetscape improvements, establishment of traffic circles, development of specialized meeting and exhibition space, provision of adequate parking, and other concerns. The master plan also aims to promote the regeneration of commercial activity in nearby derelict blocks, relieve traffic congestion, plan for gateway entrance features, and improve links between the oceanfront hotels, the retail and tourist streets, and the convention, cultural, and performing arts centers. The plan was approved in 2002, and in 2008 the first of several new parking structures was under construction. The structures will make space available for the creation of a central park and the development of the sound space for the New World Symphony, designed by Frank Gehry.

Formulating a Flexible Design Strategy for NorthPoint

The design team heading up the plan for redeveloping a 45-acre (18-ha) former railroad yard near the Charles River in Cambridge, Boston, and Somerville, Massachusetts, sought to establish a strong urban design framework to encourage creative market responses, a diversity of social interactions, and design innovations.[2] The project proposed the development of 5.2 million square feet (0.5 mil sq m) of building space in a transit-oriented, mixed-use neighborhood. CBT Architects of Boston and Toronto-based Greenberg Consultants Inc. led a group of consulting firms in fashioning a strategy with the flexibility to respond to evolving needs and market demands over time. Calling their approach "private urbanism," the design team eschewed formal designs and "product urbanism" in preparing a master plan and design guidelines for the multi-year project. Ken Greenberg, the principal of his firm, asserts that in large-scale undertakings, flexibility is the key to success. Cities evolve a rich diversity through time, he says, and "urban design should allow for this diversity and not predetermine the outcomes." Kishore Varanasi, a member of the design team, comments that designers need "to rethink what to control and what not to control, recognizing that each context—and each project—is different."[3]

The master plan conceived for this project keeps the development program constant while the mix of uses in each of the 22 developable blocks is left open to respond to the current market as development

Opposite: The master plan for Miami Beach's Convention Center District promoted regeneration of a derelict neighborhood, relieved traffic congestion, and linked numerous neighborhood venues. The Anchor Shops and parking garage sit at an intersection that had been closed to traffic for almost 40 years.

Photo: Zyscovich

occurs. Even the development phasing is adaptable to changing conditions. Indeed, the land use plan has undergone several transformations in response to market and infrastructure considerations. For example, the development of the new Green Line transit station at Lechmere Square was moved from the third to the first phase to take advantage of changes in the market and transportation improvements, opening up opportunities for timely development that contributed to the success of the project.

The design guidelines are a critical contributor to the plan's flexibility. Architects and developers often complain that design guidelines are too prescriptive, being tailored to generate predetermined forms of development. The NorthPoint guidelines have been significantly simplified to avoid prescriptive details such as setbacks, cornice lines, and proportions of certain surface materials. Furthermore, the master plan specifies that the guidelines are to be followed in spirit rather than literally. Varanasi notes that stringent guidelines are "no different than inflexible suburban zoning requirements in their ability to produce mediocre urban forms."[4] The intent is to avoid restricting the possibilities for creative design solutions. Instead, NorthPoint's design guidelines emphasize a quality-based agenda rather than simply a dimensional one, including a description of the role of each block in the plan's overall context. In effect, the blocks—each approximately an acre (0.4 ha)—and their relationship to the street

Opposite: The 22-block NorthPoint site in Cambridge, Massachusetts, is being developed as a mixed-use, transit-oriented neighborhood.

Below: NorthPoint's plan brings a human scale to the neighborhood with plentiful green space.

Photos: Jones Lang LaSalle

network became fundamental organizing elements of the urban design. Scaled to avoid the contemporary emphasis on bulky development, each block was capable of handling a variety of land uses.

Flexible plans require design attention throughout their implementation. At NorthPoint the development and consulting teams continue to collaborate, developing improvements, adapting to new ideas, and working out the concerns of public agencies.

Revitalizing Boulder's Center with a Transit Village

In September 2007, the city of Boulder, Colorado, adopted an area plan and implementation program for a transit village to guide redevelopment and revitalization of a 160-acre (65-ha), mixed-use, partially developed area in the city's center. Boulder's "area plans" bridge the gap between the broad goals of the Boulder Valley Comprehensive Plan and those of individual public and private developments. The transit village area plan provides a vision for future development, including uses, densities, and supportive community services and emphasizing special urban design qualities for transit-oriented development. An accompanying implementation plan sets out the process and timeline for various zoning and other regulatory changes, funding mechanisms, programs, and plan reviews and updates.

The area has had a checkered history, beginning with the arrival of gold prospectors and the founding of Boulder City in 1859, but was largely bypassed in Boulder's subsequent development. Functioning primarily as a rail junction, the area remained mostly rural, with a few homes and retail uses and some industries developed along the rail lines. It was also the site at various times of rail depots, racetracks, rodeo facilities, the county fairgrounds, ballparks, and other recreational lands. The nearby Crossroads Mall, developed in 1963, became Boulder's sole regional shopping center until the late 1990s. Regional centers developed in surrounding communities caused its closure in 2002, but the site was redeveloped into the lifestyle retail center called Twenty-Ninth Street; it brought new activity and stimulated the city's attention to this rather neglected area.

The area plan builds on the development prospects arising from the planned extension of bus rapid transit service to downtown Denver in the near future and the development of a new transit-oriented neighborhood on 16 acres (6.5 ha) of city-owned land along the Goose Creek greenway. The area's proximity to downtown and the Twenty-Ninth Street lifestyle center and to proposed commuter-rail service in the longer term stimulated

The city of Boulder, Colorado, has developed plans for a transit village to provide a coordinated vision for future development. Guidelines build in flexibility to allow for different building sizes, styles, and densities.

Graphic: City of Boulder

planning for long-term development. The plan describes projected development uses, densities, and supportive community services and provides design guidelines in each of eight districts within the transit village.

The plan contains a major section on urban design that describes general guidelines for the area and specific recommendations for each of the eight "character districts" within the project area. For example, the section on the Pearl Street Center District includes design guidelines for the district as a whole, for a proposed pocket park next to Goose Creek, and for transit facility features, access, loading, and parking. The plan also foresees street connectivity improvements, a

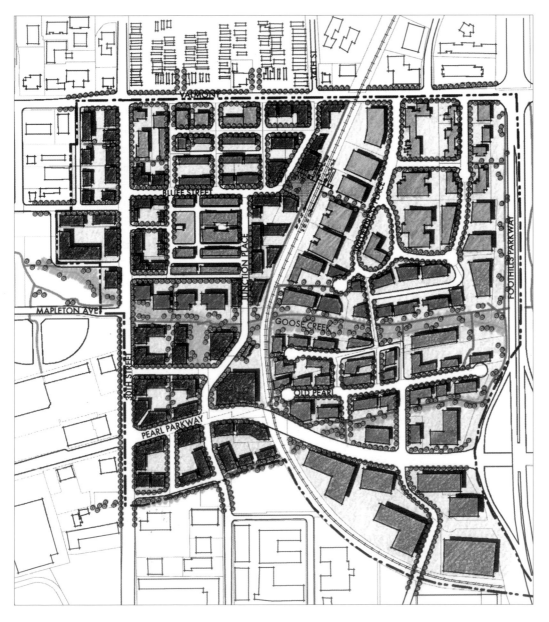

transportation demand management program, an affordable housing program, and the promotion of green building.

The city and planning board staffs developed the plan in a close working relationship with a number of design, transportation, and other consultants as well as a ULI panel's evaluation of planning and design issues. In an initial planning effort, the city engaged several architectural firms to prepare design concepts for individual sections of a much larger area. According to Louise Grauer, who managed the area planning process, the results suggested the need for a more focused plan, to provide a conceptual structure for the area's long-term development.

Designers from EDAW's Denver office were brought in to frame the issues and come up with a design plan—what the project manager, Cales Givens, describes as "constructing the context and direction for future development." After a round of stakeholder interviews, the firm conducted a three-day charrette probing topics such as open-space needs, varieties of urban form attuned to transit opportunities, and appropriate land uses. It ended with the EDAW team presenting a plan based on broad principles (reflecting the goals established earlier by the city council and planning board). The plan laid out a design structure for the area, proposed flexible approaches to development, and pointed out creative opportunities rather than block-by-block urban designs.

Givens says the plan for a primarily residential neighborhood satisfies the vision adopted by the city council and planning board, which views the Transit Village as "a place that is not overly planned, with a 'charming chaos' of building sizes, styles, and densities where not everything looks the same." The plan recognizes that most development within the area will be privately sponsored and occur over a period of two or three decades. Design details will be worked out by more focused planning in eight "character districts"—a process now underway—and by individual development proposals.

The plan was adopted by the city council in September 2007, following a huge effort by staff members and consultants to refine the broad scope of the plan that emerged from the charrette. It includes a statement of goals and objectives (for example, "Create a well-used and well-loved, pedestrian-oriented place") and chapters on land use, urban design, transportation, transportation demand management, and facilities. The urban design chapter encapsulates general guidelines (such as building placement and design, permeable street faces, and bus stop design) and design guidelines for each character district (for example, for the Pearl Street Center District, lining Pearl and 30th streets with buildings rather than parking lots and improving the North Boulder

Farmer's Ditch as a greenway trail). Best of all, the plan demonstrates the city's firm intentions to make this once-bypassed area a truly important part of the city.

Re-Visioning West Palm Beach's Downtown Development

The 2007 update of West Palm Beach's 1994 downtown master plan and development code proposed changes to address mounting concerns with the quality and massing of downtown development.[5] The city commission and the mayor selected Zyscovich Architects to evaluate the 1994 plan in light of the 40 or more active development projects begun since that time, to review regulatory policies adopted after the 1994 plan, and to propose a comprehensive master plan based on

Opposite: The master plan for West Palm Beach divided the city into several neighborhoods and developed zoning and design guidelines for each.

Graphic: Zyscovich

these findings as well as an updated market analysis. In conducting this study, we elicited significant stakeholder input to the master plan from public officials and the community at large.

West Palm Beach's downtown area was founded by Henry Flagler in 1893 as a residential community for employees of the two grand hotels he built on Palm Beach. Flagler commissioned one of the century's most respected city planners, John Nolen, to conceive a master plan. It was based on a green urban core centered on Clematis Street and connected by two public parks with the Intracoastal Waterway and Clear Lake. A city governmental center was to be situated across from two additional public parks along Clematis Street. Although Nolen's plan was not fully implemented, Clematis Street remains the city's central spine and commercial core and connects to the park terminus at its eastern end. Most historic neighborhoods were developed from the 1890s to the 1920s.

Most land in the downtown area either is used for residential purposes or sits vacant. The city's downtown development consisted mostly of low-density retail, public, and residential uses until the 1990s, when much of the Clematis Street frontage was redeveloped and the mixed-use CityPlace was built along Rosemary Avenue. As of 2008, nearly 50 projects in the downtown area were in various stages of development. Yet at least one-third of the developable acreage in downtown is not built out, offering opportunities for significant downtown growth—and the guidance of that growth. In addition, more than a quarter of land downtown is owned by the public sector, suggesting that the city can use public land resources to influence the shape and character of future development. Several large or aggregated parcels are held by single private owners—also an inducement for development.

Ongoing downtown development prompted concerns about the size, shape, and appearance of many of the buildings being constructed, which appeared to be increasingly at odds with the scale and quality of existing development and the streets and sidewalks they fronted. The form-based code that had been adopted in 1994 was geared toward small-scale developments on one or two lots. The code had not anticipated the aggregation of lots to allow larger developments and therefore had not provided sufficient setbacks or limits on the buildable area within the established forms of development. City officials wished to create a new plan reflecting the updated needs of the city to guide increased levels of development.

The master plan sets out several principles that guided the plan and zoning recommendations. In general, they propose

- Creating a sustainable downtown that improves residents' quality of life and attracts tourists by using zoning and design guidelines to reinforce the character of the city's commercial centers and distinctive neighborhoods;
- Formulating comprehensive strategies for retail development and cultural enhancement;
- Improving connectivity throughout downtown; and
- Improving streetscapes and traffic movement, in particular by using parks and other open space to strengthen the visual and physical links between centers and neighborhoods.

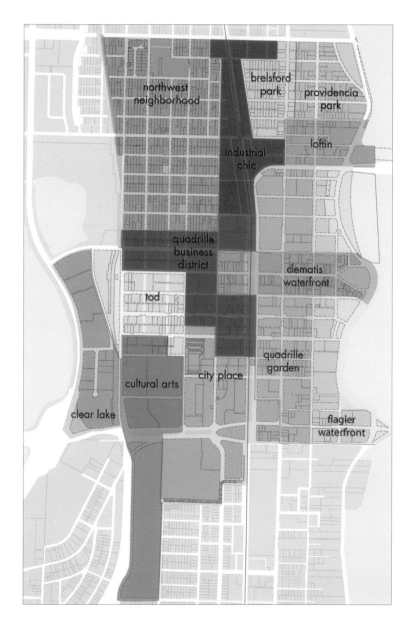

The master plan defined 14 neighborhoods within downtown that exemplified specific characteristics of existing and proposed development to be supported and enhanced by a new zoning code and architectural guidelines. In effect, each neighborhood represented a distinctive zone for regulatory purposes. Building intensities, heights, floor/area ratios, setbacks, and other code requirements and design guidelines were specified for each neighborhood. Over time, these specifications could begin to develop distinctive building scales and uses to generate a richly articulated built environment in downtown.

Floor/area ratios were proposed to replace building envelopes, encouraging more variation in building design rather than providing incentives for maximizing total square footage. Building setbacks for the

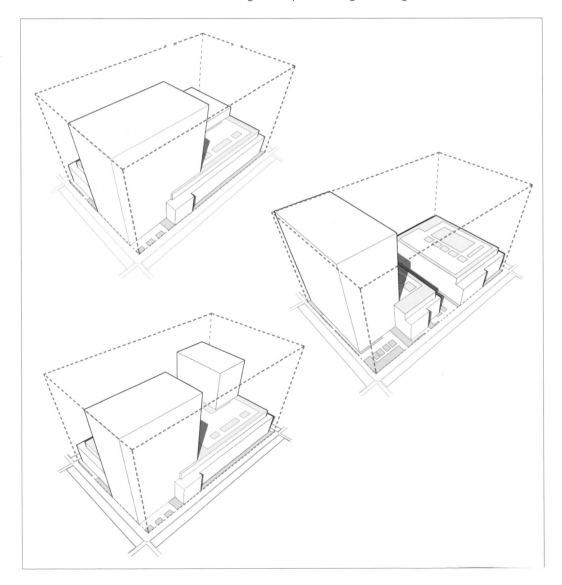

ground floor allow for wider sidewalks, encourage landscaping, and leave room for public plazas to help break the massive effects of building directly on the frontage lot line. The designation of maximum footprints on a range of lot sizes will encourage a building scale in proportion to parcel size. Creating an architectural review board to administer design guidelines for large-scale projects will help ensure a finer-grained quality of design.

Additional recommendations concerned the promotion of green building standards, more effective use of transferable development rights, the retention of historic structures, the reduction of visual impacts of parking structures, street improvements, and incentives to attract office development and affordable housing. The plan has been accepted by the commissioners and the mayor. The zoning recommendations were adopted but are now considered "zoning in progress" and will be submitted for final approval later in 2008.

Conclusion

As cities have grown in size and complexity, the negative effects of overcrowding (such as pollution and failing public services) have prompted public officials to devise regulatory regimes to guide both new development and redevelopment. These instruments of policy and practice require designers to carefully tailor project designs to the characteristics of the sites and their contexts, as well as the needs of potential users. These planning and design procedures reflect the desirable contributions of professional urban designers and planners in promoting revitalization of cities across the nation. They demonstrate the critical role of public guidance in providing a coordinating framework for urban growth and change. It is critical to keep in mind, however, that the relationship between public guidance and project design is a two-way street. Publicly adopted master plans and regulations often provide a valuable framework for specific projects, while finer-grain project design based on specific market and site circumstances can suggest alterations in public policy. In either case, the public framework should be directed to nurturing opportunities for high-quality design, which is the central goal of real urbanism.

Opposite: The city of West Palm Beach required attention to the quality and massing of its downtown development as a result of its existing form-based code.

Graphic: Zyscovich

1 Drawn from www.campuspartners.osu.edu, www.goodyclancy.com, and discussions with David Dixon, Goody Clancy's project manager.

2 Kishore Varanasi, "Private Urbanism," *Urban Land*, August 2007, pp. 65–69.

3 Varanasi, "Private Urbanism," p. 69.

4 *Ibid.*

5 "Downtown Master Plan Update," published in April 2007.

THROUGHOUT THE HISTORY of city building, the creation of iconic places such as landmark buildings, assemblies of inspiring architecture, and noteworthy green spaces has been vital to the formation of strong communities and rooted urban identities. Such places generate commerce and culture, and promote vital living environments. They provide welcoming stages for living.

America's cities are in the process of recovering from decades of decline, during which respect for urbanism had been lost. Cities are also

6 toward real urbanism

overcoming a more recent trend, the urge to copy suburbanist design prototypes. Some cities, of course, have never lost their urban forms; New York, Chicago, San Francisco, and Portland (Oregon), for example —and many international cities—remain emblematic of the excitement, convenience, and other benefits of urban living. In the late 20th century,

CityCenter Englewood in Englewood, Colorado, replaced a failing suburban mall with a mixed-use development. The project is centered on a two-acre (0.8-ha) plaza adjacent to a light-rail station.

Photo: Meeks + Partners

however, many of the nation's cities were badly affected by waning econ-omies and the flight of much of the populace to suburban enclaves. With the fading away of industry and the flight of retail activity to suburban malls, downtowns were eviscerated. In many cases, the downward spi-ral was exacerbated by ill-advised federal highway projects, and redevel-opment projects that cleared ramshackle neighborhoods only to find no takers for the vacated land. Since the mid-1990s, a reawakening of interest in urban living has generated an impressive number of redevel-opment, infill, and reuse projects in older sections of cities and growing first-tier suburbs. Designers and developers have relearned the art of building a real and dynamic urbanism.

Luohu Station is a bus, subway, and train center in Shenzhen, China, along the Hong Kong border.

Photo: Tom Fox

Recognizing Reality

Although urban designers often have chosen to adhere to a uniform, prescriptive set of codes for defining the urban qualities of development, this book proposes an alternative route to creating designs for truly urban development within cities. It champions the recognition of the special character of individual sites and development contexts as the basis for design decisions. "Getting real" about the planning and design of urban development focuses on the critical importance, first, of acknowledging the historic and current qualities of the site and its environmental, social, and economic context and, second, of creative place making that responds to these qualities and weaves new development into the existing fabric of the community. The premise of true urban design is sensitivity to the realities of the place and moment, building on and enhancing local economic and social assets. Such design aims to create truly urban places of interest to those who live and work there as well as those who pass through, places that are comfortable yet lively and constructed efficiently yet adaptable to lifelong use.

Adhering to Principles

Real urbanism also links directly with contemporary concepts for guiding development, such as smart growth, neotraditional development, sustainable development, new urbanism, and transit-oriented development. Essentially, these concepts restate the core principles that underlie the goals of the best urban designs:

Opposite and left: Bethesda Row embraces a bustling urban-style street with wide sidewalks, outdoor cafés, and neighborhood-serving stores. The creation of this pedestrian environment has put people on the sidewalks day and night and created a heart for the Bethesda downtown.

Photos: Cooper Carry

- Compact development and diversity of uses and places;
- A variety of housing, employment, and lifestyle opportunities;
- Access to choices of transportation and walkable neighborhoods;
- Efficient provision of infrastructure and public services;
- Distinctive communities with a strong sense of place;
- Preserved green spaces and other natural features; and
- Development decisions based on community involvement.

As described in chapter 2, places as different as the city of St. Louis, Missouri, and Washington, D.C.'s first-ring suburb of Bethesda, Maryland, are benefiting from imaginative designs and development based on these principles. Revitalization through urban forms of development provides space for the tasks and enjoyments of everyday life,

as well as gathering places for events, trade, and social activities. Urban designers have gained considerable experience in shaping attractive and functional masses of buildings and lively streetscapes that create appealing environments for living and working.

Park Square at Doral, Florida, is an example of a compact, diverse development, creating a distinctly urban place in this suburban city near Miami International Airport.

Graphic: Spine 3D, courtesy of Zyscovich

Aiming for Sustainable, Green Design

Urban designers are also increasingly aware of concerns about sustainability and "green" development, partly in response to the growing market demand for environmentally responsible development. Also, it is increasingly evident that environmental sustainability saves money in the long run. Buildings account for 43 percent of energy consumption in America, and we can no longer afford to ignore inefficiencies. Sustainable development presents an all-encompassing goal of keeping the world and its inhabitants alive and well. Designers tended to focus first on the preservation of green landscapes and ecosystems, the protection of wetlands and wildlife, and the promotion of the connectivity of "green infrastructure" systems throughout cities and their exurbs. Urban waterfronts have been rediscovered as attractive features, and urban designers have come to understand and attend to the social and economic implications of city development and revitalization as goals for sustainability. Many cities now provide incentives for designers to improve energy efficiency, conserve water, and wisely use and reuse materials in green buildings. Increasingly, also, designers and developers can apply a host of technical innovations that promote sustainability while enhancing living and working environments.

Park Square at Doral combines an office tower, more than 1,000 residences, and retail space lining a pedestrian plaza to create a town center.

Graphic: Spine 3D, courtesy of Zyscovich

Basing Design on Knowledge

A realistic approach to urban design pursues a process for discovery that identifies the important characteristics of the development site and its surroundings and considers the needs of future residents, workers, and visitors. The process of discovery probes the historic legacies that can guide creative revitalization and considers the past as prologue to the future. Often designers find replicable architectural and landscape features, signature buildings, visual and physical connections, and other assets that can heighten the sense of place that the new development engenders. Neighborhood studies can identify and quantify market potential for future development. Engaging the stakeholders in generating and testing design ideas early in the process can ascertain critical concerns to be addressed and achieve a shared vision for future development. Understanding the resources at hand and the interests at stake can help designers define the most advantageous qualities of proposed revitalization.

A diversity of public activities brings together people from within and around a neighborhood.

Photo: Brandon Spirk

Designing Within a Public Framework

Urban designs, no matter how visionary, must rely on a supportive framework of public policies and regulations for realization. Most cities adopt comprehensive and neighborhood plans and zoning provisions to guide development; designers must be cognizant of their implications. Planning and design firms often contribute to the public framework, either as an adjunct to plans for specific projects or through direct commissions for preparation of area plans or design-related regulatory provisions. For example, plans for revitalizing Midtown Miami in Miami, Florida, and the High Street neighborhoods in Columbus, Ohio, promoted actions by property owners, business organizations, and nonprofit groups to improve the areas. But they also included specific recommendations for zoning changes, affordable housing programs, street improvements, expansion of public parking, and other public actions.

To redevelop and maintain flourishing cities requires an understanding of and respect for their context. This book sets out the rationale for and some exemplary approaches to context-sensitive urban design. The rewards for "getting real" about urban design are distinctive, attractive, active, and economically viable urban environments for living, working, and playing.

Above: The Cap improved an area along High Street in Columbus, Ohio, bringing new vitality to the neighborhood.

Photo: Larry Hamils/Courtesy of Meleca Architecture

Opposite: Luohu Station, in Shenzhen, China, transformed 93 acres (37.5 ha) of public space into an intermodal transportation hub for the approximately 400,000 people passing through each day. Sunken gardens, pedestrian plazas, and extensive softscaping bring vibrancy to the area.

Photo: Tom Fox